PROGRAMMING LANGUAGE /ONE

Frank Bates
Mobility Systems, Inc.

Mary L. Douglas
Applied Physics Laboratory
The Johns Hopkins University

PRENTICE-HALL, INC., Englewood Cliffs, New Jersey

PRENTICE-HALL SERIES IN AUTOMATIC COMPUTATION
George Forsythe, editor

PRENTICE-HALL INTERNATIONAL, INC.,   *London*
PRENTICE-HALL OF AUSTRALIA, PTY. LTD.,   *Sydney*
PRENTICE-HALL OF CANADA, LTD.,   *Toronto*
PRENTICE-HALL OF INDIA (PRIVATE) LTD.,   *New Delhi*
PRENTICE-HALL OF JAPAN, INC.,   *Tokyo*

Library of Congress Catalog Card Number 67-17770

Printed in the United States of America

INTRODUCTION

The purposes of this book are to explain some of the techniques of using computers, and to explain the implementation of these techniques in the programming language PL/I.

Many PL/I programs appear in this book as examples to illustrate various points about the language, and about computing in general. All of the example programs have been tested on a computer (an IBM System/360); the program listings and results, where shown, are reproduced in this book directly from the printed pages produced by the computer.* The programs shown in the back of the book as solutions to the exercises have been similarly tested.

---

* Example 48 in Chapter 11 has not been tested because the necessary language features had not been implemented as of the date of publication. It is included because it illustrates principles that are essential to a full understanding of input/output facilities.

iii

PL/I was developed jointly by IBM and two organizations composed of major users of their equipment, SHARE and GUIDE. It combines many of the features of other programming languages into a single language of more general utility. Consequently, once one has learned to use PL/I effectively, he will find it easy to become proficient in other languages. Similarly, one who is familiar with other languages such as FORTRAN, ALGOL, and COBOL will find it easy to become proficient in PL/I.

ACKNOWLEDGEMENTS

Many organizations and individuals have contributed to the publication of this book. In particular, we wish to acknowledge the assistance given by The Johns Hopkins University Applied Physics Laboratory, the Union Carbide Corporation, and IBM. Additional assistance was given by Computer Applications Incorporated (New York) and the Computation Center, Stanford University.

We wish to acknowledge William T. Altmann, George S. Brown, and Carl Papa of IBM for their invaluable technical support; Jack Pendray of the U.S. Air Force for technical assistance on Chapter 11; Philip H. Dorn, Conrad H. Weisert, and Herb Van Brink of SHARE, and Dr. R. P. Rich of the Applied Physics Laboratory for reviewing the text and offering many constructive comments and suggestions; and various secretaries.

We wish especially to express our appreciation to our

editor, Dr. George E. Forsythe, Stanford University, for his

valuable ideas, advice, and encouragement.

TABLE OF CONTENTS

APPENDICES

ANSWERS TO EXERCISES

CHAPTER 1

BASIC PRINCIPLES

Electronic data processing machines (computers) are devices which perform various operations based on instructions which they have been given by the people who use them. The process of specifying a set of instructions for a computer is called programming, and the set itself is called a program.

There are two steps involved in preparing a program for a computer. First, the individual preparing the program - the programmer - must know what instructions to specify, and the sequence in which to specify them. Second, he must be able to communicate his specifications to the computer. Communication is accomplished by means of a programming "language" which the programmer writes, and the computer "reads" to decide what to do.

There are many programming languages in use today. Some are designed for very specialized applications, and some are designed for more general use. PL/I is a language in the latter category.

For a first example of a PL/I program, we will discuss a program which solves any quadratic equation of the form

$$ax^2 + bx + c = 0 \ .$$

That is, given values for a, b, and c ($a \neq 0$) the program will calculate the values of x for which the equation is satisfied. These values of x are the <u>roots</u> of the equation. The roots are obtained from the quadratic formula*

$$root1 = \frac{-b + \sqrt{b^2 - 4ac}}{2a}$$

and

$$root2 = \frac{-b - \sqrt{b^2 - 4ac}}{2a}$$

A PL/I program is made up of one or more <u>procedures</u>, which in turn are made up of <u>statements</u>. A PL/I statement is very much like a declarative or imperative sentence in English, in that it either states a property of the program or tells the computer to perform some operation or sequence of operations.

---

* The quadratic formula is not always the best way to solve a quadratic equation on a computer.

For instance, one of the statements in our program states the symbols that we will use (for example, a, b, and c); another statement tells the computer to find the value of the expression

$$\frac{-b + \sqrt{b^2 - 4ac}}{2a}$$

The application of the quadratic formula is the heart of the computation, but there are two other things our program must do. First, we must give numeric values to the coefficients (a, b, and c) before the computer can apply the quadratic formula. Second, we must include some means of getting the results out of the computer. These functions are performed by GET and PUT statements, respectively.

The program uses five <u>variables</u>, which we choose to name A, B, C, ROOT1, and ROOT2. Subject to rules described later in this chapter, we may choose any names we like for variables. It's a good idea to select names suggestive of the uses to which the variables are being put. Our program would give the same answers if its five variables were named DISTANCE, NETPAY, BBZ1, JOEBLOW, and ELEPHANTS, but the purpose of the program would be obscured.

Now, see if you can read the following program.

(Ignore the first two lines, and the last line.)

```
QUAD: PROCEDURE OPTIONS (MAIN) ;
          /* EXAMPLE NO. 1 -- COMPUTE QUADRATIC ROOTS*/

          DECLARE (A, B, C, ROOT1, ROOT2) FLOAT ;
          GET LIST(A, B, C) ;

          ROOT1 = (-B + SQRT(B**2 - 4*A*C)) / (2*A) ;
          ROOT2 = (-B - SQRT(B**2 - 4*A*C)) / (2*A) ;

          PUT LIST(A, B, C, ROOT1, ROOT2) ;

      END QUAD ;
```

Every PL/I statement ends with a semicolon, just as every English sentence ends with a period. In our example, each statement occupies one line. This format is purely for the sake of readability, and does not affect the meaning of the program. A long statement might extend over several lines, or several short statements might be placed on a single line.

Explanation of Example No. 1

QUAD: PROCEDURE OPTIONS (MAIN) ;

This is a procedure statement. It and the statements which follow form a procedure whose name is QUAD. Every program is either a single procedure like this example, or a collection of procedures. As we shall see later, the words PROCEDURE, OPTIONS, and MAIN have special significance.

4

/* EXAMPLE NO. 1 - COMPUTE QUADRATIC ROOTS */

This is a comment. It is not really a statement and it is not terminated by a semicolon. The general form of a comment is

/* anything */

where anything is a message of any length that does not contain the character pair */. No blank spaces may separate the / and the * at either end of the comment.

Comments may appear almost anywhere in a program and are ignored by the computer. They are used to aid a human reader in understanding the operation of a program. As a general rule, the more comments you use in a program, the better.

DECLARE (A, B, C, ROOT1, ROOT2) FLOAT ;

This is a DECLARE statement. In it we list the names of all the variables used in the program. The word FLOAT tells the range of values the variables may assume. DECLARE statements can be quite complicated, as Chapter 3 will show. For the moment, we can give them the general form

DECLARE (variable names separated by commas) FLOAT ;

5

It is not always necessary to list all variables in a DECLARE statement, but we recommend that you do so. It is easier to remember to put them in DECLARE statements than it is to remember when they may be left out.

GET LIST (A, B, C) ;

This <u>GET statement</u> takes three numbers in sequence from the input data* and assigns them to the variables A, B, and C, respectively.

ROOT1 = (-B + SQRT(B**2 - 4*A*C)) / (2*A) ;

This <u>assignment statement</u> computes the value of one of the roots of our equation, and gives this value to the variable ROOT1.

AN ASSIGNMENT STATEMENT IS NOT AN EQUATION, EVEN THOUGH IT LOOKS LIKE ONE. It states an action for the computer to perform, and <u>not</u> a condition of equality of the two sides. The expression on the right-hand side of the assignment operator (=) corresponds to the quadratic formula which is shown on page 3.

---

* "Input data" in general means data that can be accessed by a GET statement. The sources of input data differ among computer installations.

There is no $\sqrt{}$ symbol in PL/I; the square root function SQRT is used instead.

ROOT2 = (-B - SQRT(B**2 - 4*A*C)) / (2*A) ;

This assignment statement computes the value of the second root of our quadratic equation.

PUT LIST (A, B, C, ROOT1, ROOT2) ;

This PUT statement prints the input data (A, B, and C), and the results of our computations (ROOT1 and ROOT2). Why print the input data? There are a couple of reasons. First, it enables us to associate the answers with the proper input values. This is especially important when a program produces several hundred or thousand lines of answers rather than just one. Second, by printing the input data we can check that the numbers we read in were really the numbers we intended to read in. In a program with complicated input data it is very easy to have a few numbers missing or out of order.

The form of PUT statement we are using prints values to as many decimal places as the computer uses in doing the computation - usually between six and sixteen decimal places.

END QUAD ;

This <u>END</u> statement marks the end of procedure QUAD and the
end of our program.

Identifiers

Identifiers are used to name things in PL/I. In Example
No. 1 we used identifiers to name variables, such as A and
ROOT1; to name functions, such as SQRT; and to name the pro-
gram, QUAD, itself. Identifiers are used to name many other
PL/I entities as well.

An identifier is a combination of letters, numbers, and
underbars (or "break characters"). The first character of an
identifier must be a letter.* An identifier may not contain blanks.

These are identifiers:

    X

    A1

    VERYLONGIDENTIFIER

    W2BZB

    $_INCOME

    NET_COST

* The characters $,@, and # are considered to be letters in PL/I.

8

These are not identifiers:

RATE OF PAY	(contains blanks)
4F	(starts with a number)
F. I. C. A.	(. is neither a letter nor a number)

Keywords

Some of the identifiers used in Example No. 1 have special meanings because of the way they are used. These identifiers are called keywords. Keywords are used as names for kinds of statements, such as DECLARE; names of other program components, such as PROCEDURE, and for other purposes. As we shall see later, a given identifier may or may not be a keyword; whether it is or not depends on how it is used in a program.

The keywords used in Example No. 1 are:

PROCEDURE	GET
OPTIONS	LIST
MAIN	SQRT
DECLARE	PUT
FLOAT	END

Arithmetic Expressions

As the assignment statements in Example No. 1 show, arithmetic expressions in PL/I differ somewhat from the way

9

they are usually written in algebra. Most of the differences are
caused by the limitations of the computer equipment used for
reading and printing. For instance, exponents such as B^2 must
be written in PL/I as B**2; the numerator and denominator of a
fraction must be written on the same line, separated by a /, and
special symbols like $\sqrt{}$ must be replaced by function names.

Arithmetic expressions are made up of operators, operands,
and parentheses. In the expressions

$$A + B - 3 \quad \text{and} \quad (A - B) / 3$$

the operators are +, -, and /. The operands are A, B, and 3.

The conventional operators are

Operator	Meaning	Example
+	Addition	$a + b$
-	Subtraction or negation	$x - y$ $-b$
X or . or nothing	Multiplication	$r \times t \quad m.q \quad 4ac$
/ or ⎯ or ÷	Division	$mi/hr \quad \dfrac{a + b}{c - d}$ $p \div q$
superscript	Exponentiation	$c^2 \quad 2^n$

The corresponding PL/I operators are

Operator	Meaning	Example
+	Addition	A + B
-	Subtraction or negation	X - Y -B
*	Multiplication	R * T M*Q 4*A*C
/	Division	MI/HR (A+B)/(C-D) P/Q
**	Exponentiation	C**2 2**N

The multiplication operator * may never be omitted, as in MN for M*N. The computer must be able to distinguish between the identifier 'MN' and the expression 'M times N'. The multiplication operator must appear even when you would not expect ambiguity by leaving it out. For example, (A+B)C is illegal; the expression must be written (A+B)*C.

The strength of arithmetic operators determines the order in which operations are performed. Multiplication, for instance, is stronger than addition, so in the expression

$$A + B * C$$

the multiplication is done before the addition.

11

Strongest: ** exponentiation   -   negation (leading -)

Next strongest: * multiplication   /   division

Weakest: + addition   -   subtraction

Exponentiation and negation have equal strength, as do multiplication and division, and addition and subtraction.

Parentheses may always be used to change the order in which operations are performed.

What about the order for operations of equal strength? The rules vary for different cases. For multiplication and division, or addition and subtraction, the leftmost operation is done first. Thus,

A - B + C   means   (A - B) + C   not   A - (B + C)

and

P / Q * R   means   (P / Q) * R   not   P / (Q * R).

For exponentiation and negation, the rightmost operation is done first. Thus,

B ** POW1 ** POW2 means   B ** (POW1 ** POW2)

and

-A ** B   means   -(A ** B).

Because division and exponentiation must be written on one

line in PL/I, without use of "built-up" fractions, an expression

may need some extra parentheses. For instance,

$$\frac{a + b}{x + \dfrac{y}{z}} \qquad \text{becomes} \qquad (A + B) \ / \ (X + Y \ / \ Z)$$

$$x^{n-1} \qquad \text{becomes} \qquad X ** (N - 1)$$

Always use enough parentheses to make your meaning clear.

When in doubt, add parentheses. They never hurt.

An expression may consist of a single operand, such as

A or B or C or -3.7 or 6.

Constants

A constant is a particular form of expression. All constants

are expressions, but not all expressions are constants.

There are several different kinds of constants in PL/I,

the only ones we will use for a while are decimal numbers. A

constant may be written as an integer, with or without a sign, as

+1   0   -300000000   3244111   72037

It may be written with a decimal point, as

1.99   3.14159   -.001   007.   -1.0   0.95

13

It must, however, be a single number. 1/2 is an expression, but it is not a constant.

A third way of writing constants, called <u>scientific notation</u>, is frequently used in technical work. In scientific notation, a number is written as a decimal fraction (usually between 1 and 10), followed by 10 to some power. For example,

300000000 is written in scientific notation as 3.0×10^8

-.00000065 is written in scientific notation as -6.5×10^{-7}

The power of 10 counts the number of places the decimal point must be shifted left in the original number in order to write it in scientific notation.

Scientific notation can be used in PL/I. The letter E replaces the ' × 10' and the power of 10 follows the E. The power of 10 must be an integer constant.

3.0×10^8 is written in PL/I as 3.0E8

-6.5×10^{-7} is written in PL/I as -6.5E-7

The E may be read as "times ten-to-the". These constants all have the same value:

4.76E-2   47.600E-3   47.6E-3   0.0476E0   .0000476E3

Most computers will accept constants in the range 1E-35 to 1E35 in absolute value, and zero. Many computers will accept a much wider range.

It is important to remember two facts about arithmetic in a computer. First, a computer holds numeric values only to a fixed number of places, usually the equivalent of between 6 and 16 decimal places. (The number of digits is called the precision of a number.) For instance, a computation involving numbers of 12-digit precision will produce a result of 12-digit precision, and any low-order digits to the right of the twelfth will usually be discarded.

The second important fact is that most computers do not use base ten - that is, decimal - arithmetic internally. They may use base two, base sixteen, or some other base. This fact would be of little importance to most programmers, except for one thing: accuracy. There are fractions which, in the base-ten number system, repeat indefinitely. An example is the fraction 1/3, which is .3333... . In the same way, many fractions which can be expressed exactly in the base-ten system may turn out to be repeating fractions in the number system used by the computer. For this reason, a number like 0.1 (base ten) cannot be represented exactly in a base two computer, no matter how many digits there are.* The inaccuracy, however slight, may lead to trouble, as we will see in Chapter 4.

Arithmetic Functions

SQRT is one of many functions built into PL/I. Functions exist in PL/I to perform operations which would be difficult or laborious for programmers to describe. They usually represent small "built-in" programs.

A function may or may not have <u>arguments</u>, which are values upon which the function is to operate. In Example No. 1, for instance, the expression B**2 - 4*A*C is an argument of the SQRT function.

A function is used by writing its name followed by its arguments, if any, enclosed in parentheses. The functions we will use for the present all have numerical arguments, which may be variables, constants, or expressions. Some functions require several arguments, some require only one, and others require none. Some functions may have a variable number of arguments. Some typical PL/I functions are shown on the following page. A more complete list appears in Appendix C.

---

* $\dfrac{1}{10}$ base ten $= (\, 0.0001100110011... \,)$ base two

Function	No. of Arguments	Value	Example of Use
SQRT(X)	1	$\sqrt{X}$	SQRT(A**2 + B**2)
DATE	none	a number representing today's month, day, and year.	DATE
MAX(A, B, C)	two or more	value of largest argument.	MAX(X + Y, X/Y, 0)

Assignment Statements

Example No. 1 used two assignment statements to give
values to the variables ROOT1 and ROOT2. Assignment statements have the general form

variable name = expression ;

where

variable name is the name of a variable, i.e., an

identifier, and

expression is any expression. *

---

* The notation used here (lower case letters with an underscore)
means that a specific variable name or expression is not required,

17

THE = DOES NOT REPRESENT EQUALITY. It states
that the variable to its left is to be given a value equal to the
value of the expression in its right. That is, it states an action
to be performed, and NOT a condition of equality. Put another
way, it states that the value of the expression on the right is to
be <u>assigned</u> to the variable whose name appears on the left. The
= in an assignment statement is thus called the <u>assignment</u>
<u>operator</u>.

The following sequence of assignment statements will give
you a better idea of how they work:

X = 3 ;   (the variable X takes on the value 3)

Y = -4 ;   (Y takes on the value -4)

Z = X + Y ;   (Z takes on the value -1)

X = X + 1 ;   (X takes on the value 4)

The last statement in the sequence illustrates an important
fact about assignment statements: the expression on the right of
the assignment operator is evaluated fully before the assignment
is made to the variable on the left. Before the last statement in

---

i.e., that any variable name or expression may appear. The
items that are not underscored must appear. Thus, the general
form of the assignment statement should be read, "a variable
name followed by = followed by an expression followed by ;".

the sequence is executed, X has the value 3 (which it was given by the first of the four statements), and that is the value which is used in evaluating the expression X + 1. The result (4) is then assigned to the variable on the left, which happens to be X. The net effect of the statement, then, is to increase the value of X by one. (The effect would have been the same if the expression had been 1 + X instead of X + 1.)

What will be the value of the variable VAR (an identifier chosen arbitrarily for purposes of the example) after these two statements are executed in sequence?

> VAR = 4 ;
>
> VAR = VAR * (VAR - 1) + VAR / (VAR - 2) ;

(Answer: 14)

It is frequently convenient to assign the same value to more than one variable. This can be done in PL/I by means of a multiple assignment statement. The general form of a multiple assignment statement is

$$\underline{\text{variable}_1}, \underline{\text{variable}_2}, \ldots \underline{\text{variable}_n} = \underline{\text{expression}} ;$$

which should be read, "any number of variable names separated by commas followed by = followed by ;". For example, the statement

X, Y = 0 ;

sets the variables X and Y to zero.

The assignment statement is the fundamental operational statement in PL/I as well as in all programming languages, because it is the only way of saving a computed value. The most important thing to note about the assignment statement is that the value of the expression on the _right_ of the assignment operator is assigned to the variable on the _left_. THE ONLY THING THAT MAY APPEAR TO THE LEFT OF THE ASSIGNMENT OPERATOR IS THE NAME OF A VARIABLE, or, in the case of multiple assignment, a list of variables.

EXERCISES

1.1 Which of the following are identifiers?

A*B	IBM
A_B	VARIABLE
TIME	S360
PL/I	X1Y2
$_AMOUNT	(TEMP)
ACCOUNT-NUMBER	

1.2 Write the PL/I equivalent of the following expressions. (Example: the PL/I equivalent of a+b is A+B)

x^3 X**3

$(x-1)(x+1)$ (X-1)*(X+1)

$x^2 + 2x + 1$ X**2 + 2*X +1

$\sqrt{a^2 + b^2}$ SQRT(A**2 + B**2)

$\dfrac{a+b+c}{3}$ (A+B+C)/3

1.3 Write a PL/I program which reads two numbers representing the lengths of the legs of a right triangle and com-

21

putes the hypotenuse by means of the Pythagorean Theorem,

$$\text{hypotenuse} = \sqrt{\text{leg}_1{}^2 + \text{leg}_2{}^2}$$

[handwritten annotations in left margin:]
DECLAIR
RLT LTS? (LEG1, LEG2)
H YPOT = SQRT(LEG1**2 + LEG2**2)

1.4　Write a PL/I program which reads a number representing an employee's gross earnings and prints two values based on the earnings: a value equal to 22% of the gross pay (representing taxes), and the employee's net earnings.

1.5　Same as exercise 1.4, but use each of the following methods:

　　　a.　Determine taxes as 22% of gross pay, and net pay as 78% of gross pay.

　　　b.　Determine net pay as 78% of gross pay, and then determine the tax by subtracting the net pay from gross pay.

　　　c.　Determine taxes as 22% of gross pay, and then determine net pay by subtracting the taxes from gross pay.

　　　In each case, the sum of the two numbers (taxes, and net

22

pay) should equal the gross pay.   Can you think of any

reasons why they might not?

CHAPTER 2

LOGICAL PROGRAM STRUCTURE

Chapter 1 discussed this PL/I program, which solves a quadratic equation:

```
QUAD: PROCEDURE OPTIONS (MAIN) ;
      /* EXAMPLE NO. 1 -- COMPUTE QUADRATIC ROOTS*/

      DECLARE (A, B, C, ROOT1, ROOT2) FLOAT ;
      GET LIST(A, B, C) ;

      ROOT1 = (-B + SQRT(B**2 - 4*A*C)) / (2*A) ;
      ROOT2 = (-B - SQRT(B**2 - 4*A*C)) / (2*A) ;

      PUT LIST(A, B, C, ROOT1, ROOT2) ;

      END QUAD ;
```

Before the program can be executed on the computer, it must be translated into the computer's internal language. The translation is performed by another program called a compiler which reads the PL/I program (just as the example program reads values for the variables A, B, and C) and converts the PL/I statements into the proper computer instructions. The machine-language equivalent, or object program, is then executed to perform the operations specified in the original, or source program. Every PL/I program is thus processed in two phases: a compilation phase, and an execution phase. It is EXTREMELY important to maintain the distinction of the two phases.

Some of the statements in our program tell the compiler what instructions to generate for use during the execution phase. These are called executable statements, or simply, statements. The GET statement, the two assignment statements, and the PUT statement are the executable statements in the program. These PL/I statements are translated by the compiler into computer instructions which are to be executed. The first instruction generated by the compiler for the program is also the first instruction to be executed during the execution phase, i.e., the first of several instructions generated to direct the computer to perform the operations specified in the GET statement. The GET statement is the first physical executable statement in the program because of its position in the program, i.e., ahead of all other executable statements. The GET statement is also the first logical statement in the program because it is the first to be executed. It is important to understand that the logical sequence determines whether or not a program will operate correctly.

The PROCEDURE, DECLARE, and END statements are non-executable statements, or declarations. They tell the compiler how to generate instructions for the executable statements.

The PROCEDURE statement

QUAD: PROCEDURE OPTIONS (MAIN) ;

serves to begin a logical entity called a procedure. All subsequent PL/I statements are considered by the compiler to be contained in this procedure. After the PUT statement has been compiled, the compiler sees the statement

END QUAD ;

which signifies the end of the procedure. In our example, the END statement also signifies the end of the program. After it has been compiled, the execution phase can begin.

The DECLARE statement tells the compiler something about the properties of the variables to be used in the program. The DECLARE statement is discussed at length in Chapter 3.

During execution, operations are normally performed in the sequence that corresponds to left-to-right, top-to-bottom in the source program. Our program reads three numbers into the computer, calculates roots, and prints results. After the results are printed, execution proceeds to the point corresponding to the END statement in the source program. At that point, the program is complete, and execution is terminated.

We can diagram the logic of our program by means of a flow chart which shows the steps required to solve a quadratic equation. Three steps are required:

1. establish the coefficients,

2. compute the roots, and

3. print the results.

These three steps could be implemented in any programming language to solve a quadratic equation. Thus, we can consider programs in general as logical constructions which are imple-mented by means of programming languages.

The flow chart on the following page is a logical diagram of the process of solving a quadratic equation. To the right of the chart is the implementation of this process in PL/I.

As procedure QUAD is now written, it can solve one quadratic equation. Every time we want to solve a quadratic equation, it may be necessary to recompile the program.*

---

* The necessity for recompiling depends on the particular computer and compiler in use.

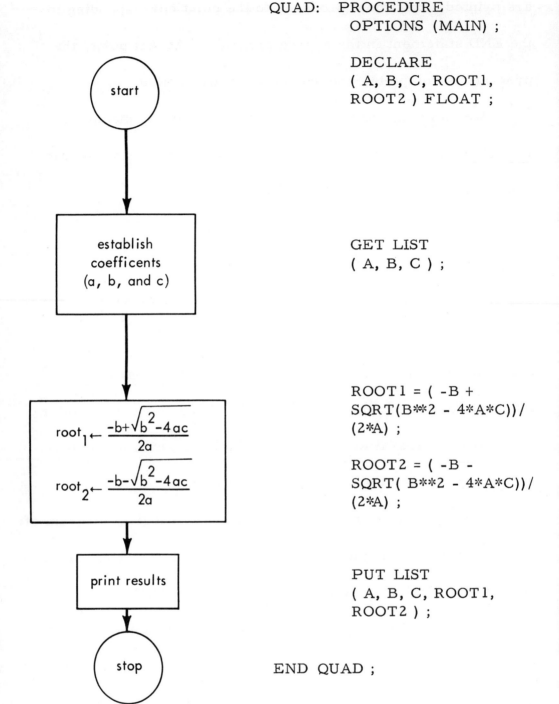

QUAD: PROCEDURE
OPTIONS (MAIN) ;

DECLARE
(A, B, C, ROOT1,
ROOT2) FLOAT ;

GET LIST
(A, B, C) ;

ROOT1 = (-B +
SQRT(B**2 - 4*A*C))/
(2*A) ;

ROOT2 = (-B -
SQRT(B**2 - 4*A*C))/
(2*A) ;

PUT LIST
(A, B, C, ROOT1,
ROOT2) ;

END QUAD ;

This approach has two great disadvantages:

1. It does not utilize the computer efficiently.
   The compilation phase may take several
   seconds, while the execution phase may take
   only a few thousandths of a second. This
   means that most of the cost (and time) of
   running the program is incurred by the non-
   productive compilation phase, while only a
   small fraction is directly connected with the
   productive work of solving the problem.

2. The time and effort required to prepare the
   program, submit it for processing on the
   computer, and receive results would probably be far greater than the time and effort
   required to solve the equation by hand.

Both of these disadvantages can be overcome by modifying
the program so that it will solve an arbitrary number of quadratic
equations, rather than just one. In other words, we want to write
a PL/I program to implement the logical construction (flow chart)
shown on the following page. The PL/I implementation of the
process is shown on page 31.

The new program (Example No. 2) is very similar to the
original program (Example No. 1). The GET statement has been
given the name START, and a GO TO statement has been inserted
following the PUT statement.

The name START in Example No. 2 is a statement label,
or, simply, a label. Labels are used to name statements in PL/I.

29

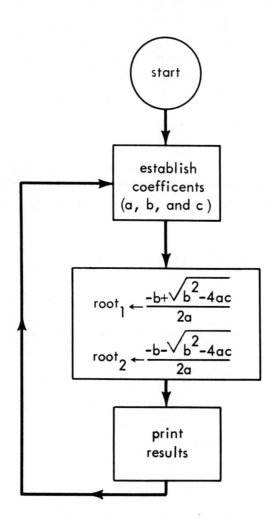

```
QUAD: PROCEDURE OPTIONS (MAIN) ;
          /* EXAMPLE NO. 2
             COMPUTE QUADRATIC ROOTS FOR ARBITRARY
             NUMBER OF CASES. */

          DECLARE (A, B, C, ROOT1, ROOT2, DISC) FLOAT ;

START:    /* EVERY SOLUTION STARTS HERE. */
          GET LIST(A, B, C) ;
          DISC = SQRT(B**2 - 4*A*C) ;
          ROOT1 = (-B + DISC) / (A+A) ;
          ROOT2 = (-B - DISC) / (A+A) ;
          PUT LIST(A, B, C, ROOT1, ROOT2) ;
          GO TO START ;
       END QUAD ;
```

Labels have the general form

<u>name</u> :

where <u>name</u> is an identifier, i.e., a combination of letters,

numbers, and underbars (break characters), the first character

of which is a letter. The colon following the name tells the

compiler that the name is being <u>defined</u> as a label. There may

be any number of blanks (or no blanks) between the name and

the colon.

A statement label is associated with the statement which

physically follows it. In Example No. 2, the label START is the

name of the GET statement. There is no significance in the fact

that the label is on a different line from the GET statement which

it names. The only restriction is that the named statement must

31

be the first statement following the label. As long as that restriction is satisfied, physical placement is arbitrary. As a general rule, it is a good idea to place labels so that they can be readily discerned by someone reading the program.

Labels are usually used to name statements so that control can be transferred to them during execution. However, labels can also be employed for documentation purposes to indicate the logical segments of the program to a human reader.

The GO TO statement used in Example No. 2 is used to alter the sequence of execution (not compilation). The general form of a GO TO statement is

GO TO label ;

where label is a statement label which is defined in the program.

GO TO statements are sometimes called "transfers". They may transfer control "forward" or "backward". In Example No. 2, the transfer is "backward", i.e., in the direction opposite to normal program flow.

In Example No. 2 the END statement cannot be executed. After the PUT statement is executed, control passes to the next statement in sequence. That statement is the GO TO statement which tells the computer to break the sequence and take its next instruction from a specified place, namely, the label START. After transferring to START (more precisely, to the statement labeled START), control resumes in the normal sequence from that point and continues until the normal sequence is again broken by the GO TO statement. The process continues as long as there are data to be read into the computer. After the last results have been printed, the program will return to the GET statement as usual, but upon sensing no more data, the computer will terminate program execution.

There are several ways in which we can modify our program so that it can decide for itself when it has processed the last set of data. For example, the quadratic formula,

$$\frac{-b \pm \sqrt{b^2 - 4ac}}{2a}$$

will not work if a is zero. (If a is zero, the quadratic formula requires division by zero, an algebraic operation which is undefined.) We can use this fact as the basis for a decision, and implement the construction shown on the following page.

The diamond-shaped block in the flow chart is called a decision block (rectangular blocks are called process blocks), and indicates that a decision is to be made. In this case, the

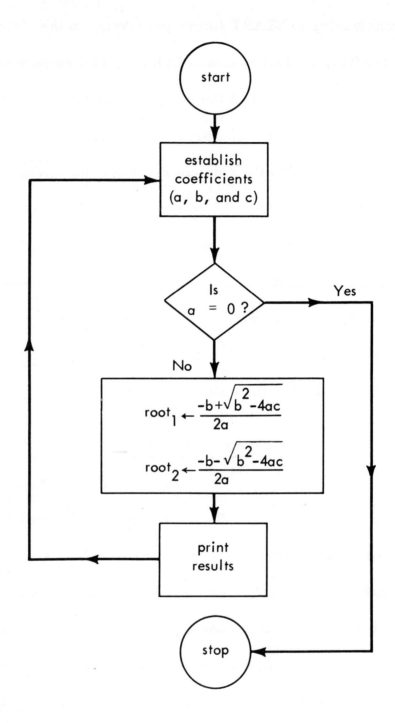

decision is to terminate program execution if the value read in

for A is zero.

Now, here is the PL/I implementation of the process:

```
QUAD:      PROCEDURE OPTIONS (MAIN) ;

           /* EXAMPLE NO. 3
              COMPUTE QUADRATIC ROOTS FOR ARBITRARY
              NUMBER OF CASES. TERMINATE EXECUTION
              WHEN THE VALUE OF 'A' IS ZERO. */

           DECLARE (A, B, C, DISC, ROOT1, ROOT2) FLOAT ;

START:     /* EVERY SOLUTION BEGINS HERE. */
           GET LIST(A, B, C) ;

           IF A=0 THEN GO TO FINISH ;

           DISC = SQRT(B**2 - 4*A*C) ;
           ROOT1 = (-B + DISC) / (A+A) ;
           ROOT2 = (-B - DISC) / (A+A) ;
           PUT LIST(A, B, C, ROOT1, ROOT2) ;
           GO TO START ;

FINISH:  END QUAD ;
```

There are two differences between Example No. 3 and the

previous examples: an **IF** statement has been inserted following

the GET statement, and a label (FINISH) has been placed on the

END statement.

After each set of data has been read in, the value of the

variable A is tested. If A is equal to zero, control is transferred

to the label FINISH, i.e., to the END statement, and execution is

terminated.

What happens if A is <u>not</u> equal to zero? The GO TO state-

35

ment is not executed; it is skipped, and execution proceeds to the calculation of the value for DISCRIMINANT. The remainder of the computation follows, and eventually the GO TO statement following the PUT statement will be executed, transferring control back to the label START. The next set of data will be read in as usual, the value of A will be tested, and control may or may not be transferred to FINISH, depending on its value.

The statement

$$\text{IF} \quad A=0 \quad \text{THEN GO TO FINISH} \;;$$

is a <u>conditional</u> transfer statement. The transfer may or may not occur, depending on a specific condition, namely, that the value of the variable A is zero. If A is equal to zero, the condition is "true", and the transfer will occur. Otherwise, the condition is "false", and the transfer will not occur.

IF statements have the general form

$$\text{IF} \quad \underline{condition} \quad \text{THEN} \quad \underline{statement} \;;$$

where <u>condition</u> describes the condition that must exist in order for <u>statement</u> to be executed. If the prescribed condition does not exist, the statement is simply skipped.

In Example No. 3, the condition is that A is equal to zero,

36

written in PL/I as A=0. The statement is GO TO FINISH.

A condition is specified in PL/I by two expressions separated by a comparison operator.* In Example No. 3, the expressions are A and the constant zero; the comparison operator is the equals sign (=), which specifies the relationship that must exist between the two expressions in order for the condition to be true.

THE EQUALS SIGN USED AS A COMPARISON OPERATOR HAS AN ENTIRELY DIFFERENT MEANING FROM THAT WHICH IT HAS WHEN USED AS AN ASSIGNMENT OPERATOR. The meaning of the symbol = is determined by the compiler from the context in which it appears in the PL/I program. It is very important to remember that in PL/I the symbol = has two distinct meanings; its meaning at any particular appearance in a PL/I program is determined by context.**

There is one set of comparison operators in PL/I, but their representation varies among computer installations. The

_____

* Also called a <u>relational operator.</u>

** In some programming languages the symbol = is used exclusively as a comparison operator. In these languages, the assignment operation is specified by symbols which are much more descriptive of the operation. Two of the more common assignment operators are ← and := . Note that we have used the symbol← in the flow charts appearing in this book.

symbols used in this book are listed below. An alternative set
appears in Appendix A.

Condition	True if ...
A ¬< B	A is not less than B
A < B	A is less than B
A <= B	A is less than or equal to B
A = B	A is equal to B
A ¬= B	A is not equal to B
A >= B	A is greater than or equal to B
A > B	A is greater than B
A ¬> B	A is not greater than B

Some conditions are equivalent. For example, the condition A<B is equivalent to B>A; A=B is equivalent to A-B=0;
and A¬<B is equivalent to A>=B.

Simple conditions can be combined into more complex conditions by means of logical operators. (These operators are
more accurately described as "bit-string operators" but for the
moment we will use them in a "logical" sense, to determine the
truth or falsity of conditions.) As with comparison operators,
the representation of the logical operators varies among computer

installations. The symbols used in this book are listed below.

An alternative set appears in Appendix A.

Symbol	Meaning
¬	NOT
&	AND
|	OR

As an example, <u>statement</u> in the following IF statement

will be executed if the expression A is equal to 3 and expression

B is greater than expression C:

IF A=3 & B>C THEN <u>statement</u> ;

We might want to execute <u>statement</u> if and only if that condition

were not true. In that case, the PL/I statement would be

IF ¬(A=3 & B>C) THEN <u>statement</u> ;

The parentheses specify that the symbol ¬ applies to the entire

condition. In other words, if the condition (A=3 & B>C) is <u>not</u>

true, then <u>statement</u> will be executed.

It must be emphasized that logical operators are used to

combine <u>conditions</u>. Sometimes, this is a very easy point to overlook. For example, if A and B are expressions and it is desired to execute a statement if either or both are equal to zero, you might be tempted to write

IF A|B=0 THEN <u>statement</u> ;

which is incorrect. The correct statement is

IF A=0 | B=0 THEN <u>statement</u> ;

An easy way to avoid such problems is to parenthesize each of the conditions to be combined. For example, the following IF statement could be used to execute a statement if the value of expression Y lies between the value of expression X and the value of expression Z (in mathematical terms, if $x<y<z$):

IF (X<Y) & (Y<Z) THEN <u>statement</u> ;

Logical operators in PL/I have the following strengths:

Strengths of Logical Operators

Strongest:	¬	"not"	(logical negation)
Next strongest:	&	"and"	(conjunction)
Weakest:	|	"or"	(disjunction)

As with arithmetic expressions, parentheses may be used in logical expressions to prescribe the order in which operations are to be performed.

The following program example reads three numbers denoting the lengths of the sides of a triangle, and sets the variable TYPE to 1 if the triangle is isosceles (two sides equal) or equilateral (all three sides equal). If the triangle is neither isosceles nor equilateral, the program sets TYPE to 0.

```
TRIANGL: PROCEDURE OPTIONS (MAIN) ;

            /* EXAMPLE NO. 4
               GIVEN SIDES OF A TRIANGLE:
               IF ISOSCELES OR EQUILATERAL, PRINT 1;
               ELSE PRINT 0. */

            DECLARE (TYPE, SIDE1, SIDE2, SIDE3) FLOAT ;
START:      GET LIST(SIDE1, SIDE2, SIDE3) ;
            IF SIDE1=0 THEN GO TO DONE ;

            /* ASSUME TRIANGLE IS NEITHER ISOSCELES NOR
               EQUILATERAL. */
            TYPE = 0 ;

            /* SET TYPE TO 1 IF NECESSARY. */
            IF (SIDE1=SIDE2)|(SIDE1=SIDE3)|(SIDE2=SIDE3)
               THEN TYPE = 1 ;

            /* PRINT DATA AND RESULTS. */
            PUT LIST(SIDE1, SIDE2, SIDE3, TYPE) ;
            GO TO START ; /* PROCESS NEXT CASE. */
DONE:       END TRIANGL ;
```

An IF statement of the form

IF <u>condition</u> THEN <u>statement</u> ;

can be illustrated by the following flow chart. <u>Statement</u> will be executed if <u>condition</u> is true, and not otherwise.

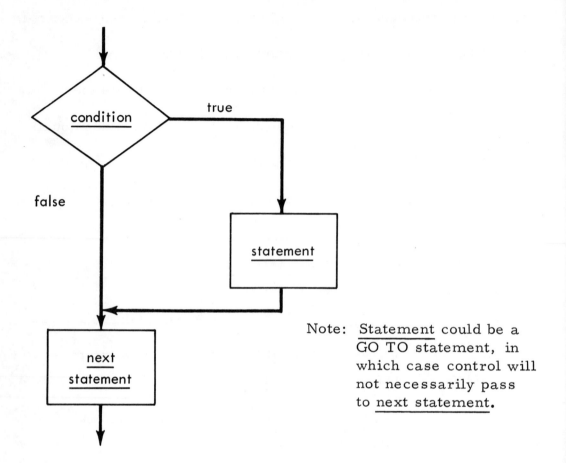

Note: <u>Statement</u> could be a <u>GO TO</u> statement, in which case control will not necessarily pass to <u>next statement</u>.

IF <u>condition</u> THEN <u>statement</u> ;

<u>next statement</u> ;

If your program requires a logical construction like that illustrated above, then you would use an IF statement of the form shown beneath the flow chart.

In addition to deciding whether or not to execute a given

statement, the IF statement can be used to decide which one of two alternative statements is to be executed, i.e., to implement the logical construction shown below. The IF statement required for the implementation is shown beneath the flow chart.

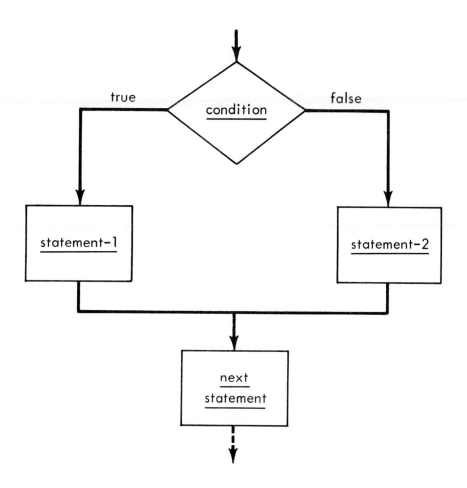

IF condition THEN statement-1 ;

ELSE statement-2 ;

next statement ;

43

This form of the IF statement specifies that if the condition is true when it is evaluated, statement-1 is to be executed. Otherwise, statement-2 is to be executed. One or the other will be executed; the two are mutually exclusive.

The following program reads two numbers and prints them out such that the larger of the two numbers is printed first.

```
SORT: PROCEDURE OPTIONS (MAIN) ;

          /* EXAMPLE NO. 5
             GIVEN TWO NUMBERS, PLACE THE LARGER IN
             'BIG' AND THE SMALLER IN 'SMALL'. */

          DECLARE (X, Y,   /* THE TWO NUMBERS */
                   BIG, SMALL) FLOAT ;

START:    GET LIST(X, Y) ;

          IF X>Y THEN BIG = X ;
                 ELSE BIG = Y ;

          IF X>Y THEN SMALL = Y ;
                 ELSE SMALL = X ;

          PUT LIST(X, Y, BIG, SMALL) ;
          GO TO START ;
      END SORT ;
```

The "ELSE-form" of the IF statement can be expanded to govern execution of any number of alternative statements, rather than just two. The flow chart on the following page illustrates one such construction, and the IF statement which follows it illustrates its implementation in PL/I.

The indentation used in the IF statement is intended to emphasize the logical construction implemented by the statement.

44

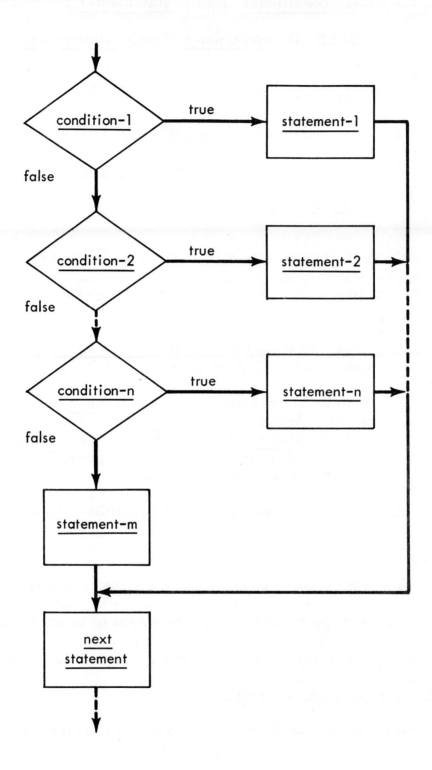

IF   condition-1   THEN   statement-1 ;

ELSE   IF   condition-2   THEN   statement-2 ;

.
.
.

ELSE   IF   condition-n   THEN   statement-n ;

ELSE   statement-m ;

next statement ;

One way to analyze a relatively complex IF statement like
this is to examine it from bottom to top, step-by-step:

1.   Under what conditions will statement-m be
     executed? (What happens if condition-n is true?)

2.   Under what conditions will condition-n be eval-
     uated? Answer: if condition-2 is false. If it
     is true, statement-2 will be executed instead;
     the IF-ELSE construction always presents
     mutually exclusive alternatives.

3.   Under what conditions will condition-2 be eval-
     uated?

It is worth noting in passing that the first condition found

to be true causes the corresponding statement to be executed; the

ELSE-path is not taken, and consequently any conditions which lie

in that ELSE-path are not evaluated.

This statement could be used to place the largest of three

values, A, B, and C, into BIG:

```
IF (A>B) & (A>C) THEN BIG = A ;
ELSE IF B>C THEN BIG = B ;
      ELSE BIG = C ;
```

The following flow chart is similar, but not identical, to the preceding one. Here, it is possible for none of the alternatives to be executed.

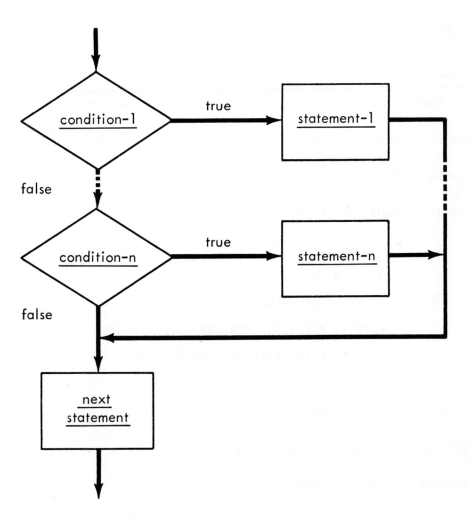

IF   condition-1   THEN   statement-1 ;

.

.

.

ELSE   IF   condition-n   THEN   statement-n ;

next statement ;

The above statement differs from the previous one in that it specifies no alternative (ELSE) for the last IF statement contained in it. If, in the above statement, condition-n is not true, statement-n is skipped; in any case control then passes to next statement.

The following statements could be used as part of a payroll program to compute federal income tax to be withheld. It is assumed that the most common withholding figure is 20%, so the figure is initially set to 0.20 and modified only if necessary.

```
TAX = 0.20 ;
IF PAY>1400 THEN TAX = 0.30 ;
ELSE IF PAY>1200 THEN TAX = 0.25 ;
    ELSE IF PAY>1000 THEN TAX = 0.23 ;
```

You may have noticed from the preceding illustrations that ELSE, if used, specifies an alternative path to be taken if the last preceding condition is false. In PL/I, that is in fact the rule:

48

<u>ELSE</u>, if used, specifies an alternative path for

the last preceding <u>IF</u> for which an <u>ELSE</u> path is

not already specified.

The following flow chart and statement illustrate the rule.

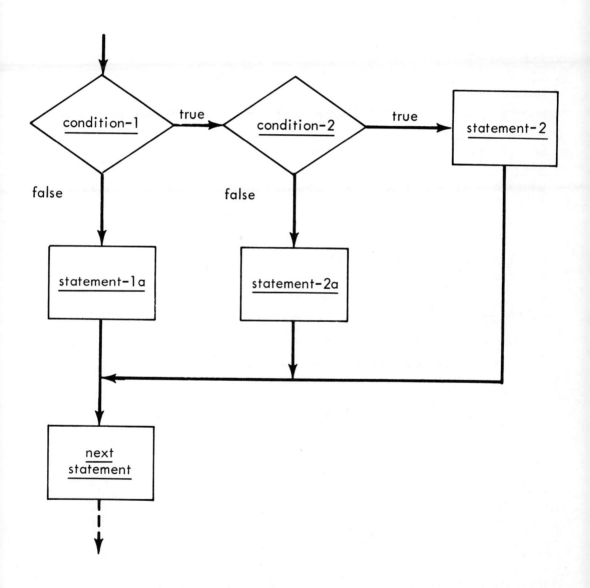

```
IF  condition-1  THEN

    IF  condition-2  THEN  statement-2 ;

    ELSE  statement-2a ;

ELSE  statement-1a ;

next statement ;
```

A typical application of this kind of IF statement might be as follows. Assume an employer allows his employees a certain number (S) of "sick days" per year. Employees who have a perfect attendance record receive an extra day of vacation, but those who were absent more than the allowable number of sick days are docked the excess. The employer could use the following statement to compute the number of vacation days due an employee:

```
IF ABSENCES < S THEN
    IF ABSENCES = 0 THEN VACATION = VACATION + 1 ;
    ELSE ;
ELSE VACATION = VACATION - (ABSENCES - S) ;
```

The construction

```
ELSE ;
```

appearing in the preceding IF statement is an example of a null statement. It specifies that if the last preceding condition is false then no operations are to be performed. A null ELSE path is needed here so that the following ELSE will be taken as the alternative for the first IF. Remember that ELSE, if used, is always associated with the last preceding IF for which an ELSE path was not specified. In other words, if we need an ELSE path for an outer IF, we must first have ELSE paths for all of the inner IFs. As in the preceding statement, some of these paths may be null paths.

The construction

(a)   IF condition THEN statement ;

       ELSE ;

is equivalent to the construction

(b)   IF condition THEN statement ;

which is the first kind of IF statement discussed in this chapter. Indeed, form (a) can be used anywhere that form (b) could be used and the operation of the program would be the same. The converse, however, is not true. Form (a) must be used when an IF statement is "nested" within another IF statement and it is necessary to specify an ELSE path for one of the outer IFs.

The IF statements used so far have been used to decide whether or not a single statement is to be executed, or which one of a set of alternative single statements is to be executed. Often, you will find it necessary - or convenient - for an IF statement to govern the execution (or non-execution) of a group of statements, rather than just one.

A group of statements is begun in PL/I by the DO statement, which has the form

DO ;

and is terminated by an END statement.* The DO statement, the END statement, and any statements in between comprise a DO group. As shown in the following example, a DO group behaves much like a single statement.

Example No. 5 (page 44) read two numbers and placed the larger in BIG and the smaller in SMALL by using two IF statements. By using an IF statement to govern the execution of more than one statement we can do the same thing by implementing the construction shown on the next page.

---

* The DO statement can be used in a different form to specify that the group of statements is to be executed repeatedly. This use of the DO statement is described in Chapter 4.

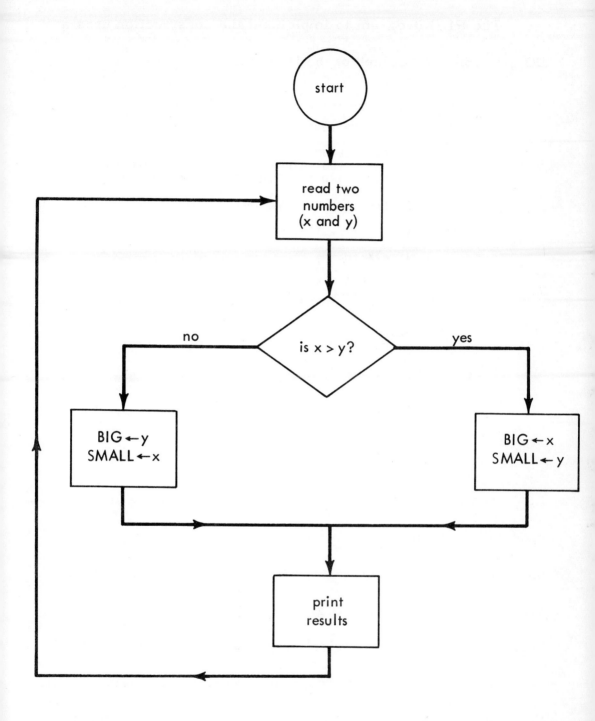

The PL/I program to implement the construction uses a DO group in each branch of the IF statement:

```
SORT: PROCEDURE OPTIONS (MAIN) ;
          /* EXAMPLE NO. 6
             GIVEN TWO NUMBERS, PLACE THE LARGER IN
             'BIG' AND THE SMALLER IN 'SMALL'. */

          DECLARE (X, Y, BIG, SMALL) FLOAT ;
START:    GET LIST(X, Y) ;
          IF X>Y THEN
             DO ;
                BIG = X ;
                SMALL = Y ;
             END ;

          ELSE
             DO ;
                BIG = Y ;
                SMALL = X ;
             END ;

          PUT LIST(X, Y, BIG, SMALL) ;
          GO TO START ;
       END SORT ;
```

The DO statement, which in the present context is a non-executable statement, serves to begin a logical entity, just as does the procedure declaration in the first line of the example. In the present case, the DO groups are logical entities (groups) "nested" within another logical entity (the procedure, SORT).

In order for the DO groups to be <u>executed</u> as logical entities, the compiler must be told when to end them; that is the function of the END statements. The END statements in the DO groups in Example No. 6 serve to terminate only the DO groups; they do

54

not terminate the larger entity, the procedure. Two general

rules are

1. Every logical entity must be terminated by an END
   statement.

2. An END statement matches the last previous DO or
   PROCEDURE statement.

There may be any number of statements in a DO group,

but the principle is always the same: the group is executed or

skipped as a whole. A DO group containing a single statement

behaves in exactly the same way as would the statement by itself.

Some of the statements in a DO group may be IF statements,

and the statements governed by the conditions in those IF state-

ments may also be DO groups.

Note the indentation used in Example No. 6. The particu-

lar indentation in the example is used to emphasize the logical

structure of the program, to make it easier to read and under-

stand what it is supposed to do. The same results would be

obtained if the statement had been written

```
IF X<Y THEN DO;BIG=X;SMALL=Y;END;ELSE DO;BIG=Y;SMALL=X;END;
```

but the logical structure of the program would have been obscured.

Most cases of improper results can be traced to errors in logical program structure. Almost every program has such "bugs" which must be located and fixed before the program can be used successfully. You will find it extremely helpful to emphasize the logical structure of your programs wherever possible in order to simplify the inevitable problem of finding logical errors or oversights ("debugging"). The indentation used in Example No. 6, for instance, shows at a glance that the DO groups are associated with a particular decision. That same glance can determine the contents, or scope of the groups.

This chapter has introduced the concept of a computer program as a logical construction. PL/I is one particular language used to communicate with the computer, just as English is one particular language used to communicate with people. There is not necessarily any correlation between the physical appearance of a PL/I program and the logical construction it represents, but it is essential to remember that it is the logical construction that determines whether a program will produce the desired results.

GO TO (transfer) and IF (decision) statements are two of the most powerful statements in PL/I. They can be used to express complicated logical constructions very simply.

There are three basic forms of the IF statement. When you set out to solve a problem on a computer you will first formulate the logical construction representing the solution, and then write the appropriate statements to express that construction to the computer. The form of IF statements you use should be the one that makes for the simplest program; there is no generally "preferable" form.

Note on Conditions

The algebra of logic, known as Boolean algebra, is concerned with two values: "true" and "false." In PL/I, "true" is represented as the quantity 1 (one) and "false" is represented as the quantity 0 (zero). Every condition in PL/I yields one of these values when it is evaluated.

Because the values resulting from the evaluation of conditions (logical expressions) are numeric (0 or 1), logical expressions can be used in arithmetic expressions.* For example, a company preparing monthly statements for its customers may wish to indicate a balance due for those accounts in which current charges exceed the current amount in the

---

* Thus, conditions are not at all restricted to use with IF statements.

account; otherwise, the statements are to show a balance due of zero. The following statement might appear in the PL/I program used to prepare the statements:

```
BALANCE_DUE = (CHARGES>DEPOSITS)*(CHARGES-DEPOSITS) ;
```

This statement is an assignment statement which assigns a value to the variable named BALANCE_DUE. As in all assignment statements, the expression to the right of the assignment operator (=) is evaluated before the assignment is made. In this case, there are two expressions to the right of the assignment operator: a logical expression, or condition (CHARGES> DEPOSITS), and an arithmetic expression (CHARGES - DEPOSITS). The asterisk, of course, specifies that the values of the two expressions are to be multiplied together.

The logical expression (CHARGES>DEPOSITS) yields a value of 0 or 1; the value is 1 if CHARGES has a value greater than that of DEPOSITS. Otherwise, the value is 0. In other words, the expression has a value of 1 if there is a balance due, else 0.

The entire expression on the right side of the assignment operator then evaluates to either

0*(CHARGES-DEPOSITS)   or zero

or

1*(CHARGES-DEPOSITS)   or the amount due,

and the resulting value is then assigned to the variable named

BALANCE_DUE.

2.1   The variable named DISC in Example No. 3 (page 35)

is not really necessary, because it could be replaced

by the expression B**2 - 4*A*C at each appearance.

Furthermore, if DISC were not used, an assignment

statement would be eliminated from the program, thus

making the program physically shorter. What advant-

ages, if any, are gained by using this "extra" variable

in the program?

2.2   Given the following three sets of data:

1)	A = 10	B = 5	C = 0
2)	A = 0	B = 10	C = 5
3)	A = 5	B ≐ 0	C = 10

For each set of data, what value will be printed by each of

the two PUT statements shown on the following page?

```
1)              IF A>B THEN R = 1 ;
                IF B>C THEN R = 2 ;
                IF A>C THEN R = 3 ;

                PUT LIST( R ) ;


2)              IF A>B THEN R = 1 ;
        ELSE IF B>C THEN R = 2 ;
        ELSE IF A>C THEN R = 3 ;

                PUT LIST( R ) ;
```

2.3   Write a PL/I program which reads three numbers and

prints results as follows:

0   if the numbers do not represent the sides of a
         triangle.

1   if they represent the sides of a triangle which
         is neither isosceles nor equilateral.

2   if they represent the sides of an isosceles
         triangle.

3   if they represent the sides of an equilateral
         triangle.

Write the program so that it will process an arbitrary

number of sets of three numbers, and will terminate upon

reading a set of three numbers, all of which are 0.

(Assume that all non-zero data will be positive.)

2.4　Modify the program written for exercise 2.3 so that it will

print the following additional values:

4　　　if the triangle is a right triangle, but is not
　　　　isosceles.

5　　　if the triangle is a right isosceles triangle.

(Hint:　First, find the longest side, then determine if its
square is equal to the sum of the squares of the other two
sides.)

2.5　The equals sign (=) has two different meanings in PL/I.

It can specify assignment, and it can specify the relation-

ship that must exist between two expressions in order for

a condition to be true.　Is the statement

$$A = B = C ;$$

a legal PL/I statement?　If so, what will happen when it

is executed?

CHAPTER 3

ATTRIBUTES

In the program examples in previous chapters all data
items have been arithmetic (numeric) but PL/I permits other
kinds of data as well; for example, strings of alphabetic characters.

There are three kinds of data with which we will be concerned throughout this book:

1. Arithmetic data,

2. String data, and

3. Label data.

The characteristics of data are called <u>attributes</u>. Attributes may be specified explicitly by including them in DECLARE
statements, or "by default" by omitting them from DECLARE
statements.

In all cases, data items may be constants, or variables.
Constants are specified by writing their <u>values</u> each time they

are to be used. The form in which they are written determines their attributes.

Variables are used by writing their names each time they are to be used. The attributes of variables are specified in DECLARE statements before the names are used. The declared attributes remain the same throughout the program.

Certain attributes are applicable only to certain kinds of data. For example, we can specify the precision of arithmetic data, and the length of a character string, i.e., how many characters it contains, but it is meaningless to specify the "precision" of a character string.

The general form of a DECLARE statement is

DECLARE name attributes ;

where name is an identifier and attributes specify its characteristics.

Usually, several identifiers will have the same attributes. In such cases, the attributes can be "factored" to reduce the amount of writing required. The general form of a DECLARE statement with factored attributes is

DECLARE (name-1, name-2, ...) attributes ;

which is similar to the first form, except that the names are separated by commas and the list is enclosed in parentheses.

Arithmetic Data

Arithmetic data items have numeric values. The range of values that an item can assume and the form in which these values are maintained inside the computer can be specified in a DECLARE statement.

In order to understand the range of values that an arithmetic data item can assume, it may be helpful to think of an item as a box into which a specified number of digits can be placed. Suppose, for example, that each arithmetic data item can hold six decimal digits.* The range of numeric values that each item can assume then depends on the position of the decimal point.

Range	Arithmetic Data Item (6 digits)
0 to 999999 in steps of 1	decimal point
0 to 9999.99 in steps of 0.01	
0 to .999999 in steps of .000001	

---
* In the computer, the item might have a sign (+ or -), too.

65

The range of values, as well as the resolution (the smallest detectable difference between two values) depends entirely upon the position of the decimal point. If the position is specified, the data item is called a fixed-point quantity. For example, if the item is to be used in calculations involving dollars and cents, it would be specified as fixed-point with two digits to the right of the decimal point (as in the second illustration on the preceding page).

When the decimal point is at the right-hand end of the data item, as in the first illustration, the item is called an integer. Integers are a special case of fixed-point numbers; the value of an integer is always a whole number.

The general form of specifying the characteristics of a fixed-point arithmetic data item is

DECLARE name FIXED (p, q) ;

where

name is the name of the item (an identifier),

p is the number of digits in the item ("the size of the box"), and

q is the number of digits to the right of the decimal point.

$\underline{p}$ is called the $\underline{precision\ attribute}$.

The three illustrations on page 65 reflect the following

three DECLARE statements:

DECLARE $\underline{name}$ FIXED (6, 0) ;

DECLARE $\underline{name}$ FIXED (6, 2) ;

DECLARE $\underline{name}$ FIXED (6, 6) ;

The first DECLARE statement declares $\underline{name}$ to be an

integer. When declaring an integer, the number of digits to

the right of the decimal point (always zero) need not be speci-

fied. The statement could have been written

DECLARE $\underline{name}$ FIXED (6) ;

In the case of integers, it is not even necessary to specify

the number of digits unless there is some particular reason for

doing so. Thus, the statement could be shortened to

DECLARE $\underline{name}$ FIXED ;

and the number of digits would be determined by the particular

computer in use.

The second and third DECLARE statements declare $\underline{name}$

to be a fixed-point item other than an integer, because they specify that 2 and 6 digits, respectively, are to follow the decimal point. If the number of digits following the decimal point is specified, the number of digits in the entire item must also be specified.

The smallest absolute value, except for zero, that a six-digit data item may assume is 0.000001, and the largest is 999999. However, as the illustrations on page 65 show, this range cannot be realized if the position of the decimal point is fixed. For small numbers, the decimal point must be toward the left-hand end of the number; for large numbers, it must be toward the right. In order to maximize the range of values the item can assume, the decimal point must be permitted to "float."

The general form of specifying a floating-point item is

DECLARE name FLOAT (p) ;

where

name is the name of the item (an identifier), and

p is the number of digits.

As in the case of fixed-point items, it is not necessary to specify the number of digits unless there is some particular reason for doing so. When the number of digits is not specified, i.e., given a DECLARE statement of the form

DECLARE name FLOAT ;

the number of digits would be determined by the particular computer in use, typically between 6 and 16.

FLOAT and FIXED are called scale attributes. Every arithmetic data item must have one or the other of these attributes. FIXED specifies that the decimal point is to be fixed at some specified position in the item. FLOAT specifies that the decimal point is to be moved automatically by the computer so that the item can assume the widest possible range of values.

For illustrative purposes, it has been assumed that arithmetic data items contain decimal digits, and that the FIXED, FLOAT, and precision attributes apply to the positioning of a decimal point. In most computers, numeric values are represented internally to some base other than decimal (base ten), usually binary (base two).* The base of arithmetic data items is specified in DECLARE statements by means of a base attribute. The two base attributes in PL/I are BINARY and DECIMAL.

---

* An excellent explanation of non-decimal number systems and arithmetic can be found in An Introduction to Digital Computing by Bruce Arden, Addison-Wesley, 1963, Chapter 7.

When numeric values are in binary form, the scale and precision attributes apply to the positioning of a <u>binary</u> point.

<u>Examples</u>

DECLARE (A, B, C) FIXED DECIMAL (4, 2) ;

specifies that the variables A, B, and C are decimal arithmetic data items which can contain numbers of the form

dd. dd

where d represents a decimal digit (0 through 9).

DECLARE (X, Y) FIXED BINARY (5, 1) ;

specifies that the variables X and Y are binary arithmetic data items which can contain numbers of the form

bbbb. b

where b represents a binary digit (0 or 1).

You can think of the base attributes (DECIMAL and BINARY) as modifiers of the corresponding precision attribute:

they tell whether the precision attribute specifies the number of decimal or the number of binary digits in the item. They also tell whether the "point" (if specified) is a decimal or a binary point.

In many cases you will not be concerned with the bases of the quantities used in computation. Two plus two equals four, regardless of the base in which the quantities are represented. Thus, a DECLARE statement of the form

DECLARE name FLOAT ;

or

DECLARE name FIXED ;

may be quite satisfactory for your purposes.* However, if you find it necessary to specify a precision attribute, you should also specify a base attribute to tell the computer whether the precision attribute means binary digits (bits) or decimal digits. For example, if an arithmetic data item is to be used in calculations involving dollars and cents, it is important for the item to have two decimal digits to the right of the decimal point, and you would need a DECLARE statement of the form

---

* In general, the computation will proceed somewhat faster when the BINARY base is specified.

$$\text{DECLARE } \underline{\text{name}} \text{ FIXED DECIMAL (} \underline{n}, 2 \text{) ;}$$

where $\underline{n}$ is an integer constant which you would specify, based on the largest value that $\underline{name}$ can assume, i.e., the maximum number of digits that it must hold.

Chapter 1 indicated that it is not always necessary to list the names of variables in DECLARE statements (although it is good practice to do so). When arithmetic variables which are used in a program do not appear in a DECLARE statement the attributes are "declared by default" as follows:

1. If the first character of a name is I, J, K, L, M, or N, the scale is FIXED and the base is BINARY.

2. If the first character of a name is other than I, J, K, L, M, or N the scale is FLOAT and the base is DECIMAL.

In both cases, the precision is determined by the particular computer in use, and will be the same as if the item had appeared in a DECLARE statement without a specified precision attribute.

If a DECLARE statement specifies only the scale attribute for an item, the base is assumed to be DECIMAL.

If a DECLARE statement specifies only the base attribute for an item, the scale is assumed to be FLOAT.

72

A good way to avoid running afoul of the rules is to specify every desired attribute for each item. This practice will prevent the compiler from assuming a decimal base, for example, when you really wanted a binary base, and will make your programs easier to read. It is at least as easy to specify all of the attributes for items as it is to remember what happens when some of them are omitted.

The PICTURE attribute is another way to specify the form of arithmetic data items. The PICTURE attribute defines the form of arithmetic items by means of a symbolic representation or "picture" of their contents.

The PICTURE attribute consists of a string of "specification characters," each of which specifies the permissible contents of a digit position in the associated item(s). The present discussion will be limited to a description of only a few of these specification characters, and will show only how various item characteristics can be specified either by scale, base, and precision attributes; or by the PICTURE attribute.

Note: The PICTURE attribute cannot be used in conjunction with scale, base, and/or precision attributes.

The general form of a DECLARE statement with a
PICTURE specification is

DECLARE name PICTURE 'specifications' ;

where

name is the name of the item (an identifier), and

specifications is a string of characters enclosed in

a pair of single quote marks.

The specification character '9' specifies that the corresponding position in the item can contain a decimal digit. The
character 'V' is used to indicate that a decimal point should be
assumed to appear between the digits to either side of the 'V'.

The following pairs of DECLARE statements are equivalent:

DECLARE name FIXED DECIMAL (10) ;

DECLARE name PICTURE '9999999999' ;

DECLARE name FIXED DECIMAL (5, 2) ;

DECLARE name PICTURE '999V99' ;

The character 'F' is used to modify the position of the
decimal point. The parenthesized number following the 'F'
specifies the number of positions the decimal point should be

74

shifted to the left (a negative number specifies a shift to the right) from its assumed position. The following four DECLARE statements are equivalent:

DECLARE name FIXED DECIMAL (5, 2) ;

DECLARE name PICTURE '999V99' ;

DECLARE name PICTURE '99999F(2)' ;

DECLARE name PICTURE 'V99999F(-3)' ;

There are, of course, many other ways in which a PICTURE specification could be written to specify the same form of the data.

A "replication factor" can be used to reduce the amount of writing necessary to specify a PICTURE. A replication factor is a decimal integer constant enclosed in parentheses preceding the PICTURE character that is to be repeated. The following three DECLARE statements are equivalent:

DECLARE name FIXED DECIMAL (16, 3) ;

DECLARE name PICTURE '9999999999999V999' ;

DECLARE name PICTURE '(16)9F(3)' ;

PICTURE specifications may also be used to specify the form in which the values of arithmetic data items are to be edited for printing. The use of PICTURE for this purpose is discussed in Chapter 6, Input/Output.

It is important to note that a PICTURE specification may not contain more than one 'V' or 'F'.

Equivalent characteristics for arithmetic data items can be specified either by the scale, base, and precision attributes; or by a PICTURE specification. When specified by means of a PICTURE specification, however, computation will proceed much more slowly than it would if the individual attributes were explicitly specified. For this reason, it is far better to use the scale, base, and precision attributes when declaring arithmetic data items.

String Data

String data items are constants or variables whose "value" is a string of characters or a string of bits. A character string can contain any characters, including alphabetic, numeric, and special characters. A bit string can contain only the binary digits 0 and 1.

Character strings have two attributes: the CHARACTER attribute, which specifies a character string; and a length attribute, which specifies the number of characters in the string.

The general form of a character string constant is

'string'

where <u>string</u> is a sequence of characters. The quote marks
bracketing the string specify a character string; the number of
characters between the quote marks specifies its length. If a
string is to <u>contain</u> a quote mark, that quote mark is written as
two consecutive quote marks within the string.*

The string '' (two consecutive quote marks) is the <u>null</u>
<u>string</u>; its length is zero.

<u>Examples</u>

```
'THIS IS A STRING OF LENGTH 29'
'DUNN & BRADSTREET'
'/* THIS ISN''T A COMMENT */'
'12345.67'
```

One of the most important points to note is that blanks are
significant in character string constants. Blanks are considered
to be characters like any other. In fact, a character string can

---

* Thus, '''' is a character string constant of length 1; it contains
a single quote mark. The first and last quote marks delimit the
string, and the two central quote marks represent the <u>contained</u>
quote mark.

consist of nothing but blanks, if desired. In that case, it would be written as two quote marks, separated by the appropriate number of blank spaces.

Another way to write a character string constant is to precede the constant with a replication factor. As mentioned in the discussion of the PICTURE attribute, a replication factor is a decimal integer constant enclosed within parentheses. The notation

(10)' '

specifies a character string constant containing ten blanks. The following constants are identical in value:

'ABCABCABC'
(3)'ABC'

Character string constants can be used in PUT statements to print out alphameric information. For instance, to indicate that the end of the program was reached, the following statement might be placed just before the END statement:

PUT LIST('END OF JOB') ;

Character string variables must appear in a DECLARE statement before they are used in a program. (Otherwise, they are declared by default to be arithmetic, as mentioned in the discussion of arithmetic data.) The general form of specifying a character string variable is

DECLARE name CHARACTER (length) ;

where

name is the name of the variable (an identifier), and

length is the number of characters that name will contain.

Input data items to be assigned to variables with the CHARACTER attribute must be bracketed by quote marks, i.e., they must be character string constants.

The PL/I program on the following page will read four-letter groups of characters from the input medium, count the number of times the group "PL/I" appears, and will print that number upon reading the four-letter group "STOP".

```
COUNT:      PROCEDURE OPTIONS (MAIN) ;
            /* EXAMPLE NO. 7
               READ FOUR-CHARACTER GROUPS AND COUNT THE
               NUMBER OF APPEARANCES OF 'PL/I'. PRINT
               RESULTS UPON READING THE GROUP 'STOP'. */

            DECLARE GROUP CHARACTER(4),
                    APPEARANCES FIXED ;

            APPEARANCES = 0 ;  /* INITIALIZE THE COUNT. */
START:      GET LIST( GROUP ) ;
            IF GROUP='STOP' THEN GO TO STOP ;
            /* NOTE THAT THE CHARACTER STRING 'STOP'
               AND THE LABEL STOP ARE ENTIRELY
               UNRELATED. */
            IF GROUP='PL/I' THEN
               APPEARANCES = APPEARANCES + 1 ;
            GO TO START ;

STOP:       PUT LIST( '''PL/I'' APPEARED ',
                    APPEARANCES, ' TIMES.' ) ;
            END COUNT ;
```

Sometimes, the length of a character string variable will

not be known because it will change from time to time. For

instance, when processing a mailing list, the character strings

representing names and addresses may be of varying lengths.

A character string variable may be given the VARYING attribute

in a DECLARE statement, in which case the length specification

specifies the maximum length of the string. The statement

```
DECLARE ( NAME, ADDRESS ) CHARACTER ( 20 ) VARYING ;
```

specifies that NAME and ADDRESS are character strings of varying length, each containing at most 20 characters.

When working with character strings of varying length, it is frequently useful to know how many characters are in the string at any given time. PL/I contains a built-in function, LENGTH, which returns an integer value which is the number of characters in the string. The following program will read an arbitrary number of words (character string constants) from the input medium and print only those consisting of five characters. The program will terminate when it reads a one-character string containing a zero.

```
PRINT5:   PROCEDURE OPTIONS (MAIN) ;
          /* EXAMPLE NO. 8
             READ CHARACTER GROUPS AND PRINT ONLY THE
             FIVE-CHARACTER GROUPS. TERMINATE UPON
             READING A ONE-CHARACTER STRING CONSISTING
             OF A ZERO. */

          DECLARE STRING CHARACTER(20) VARYING,
                  CHARS FIXED ;
          /* GROUPS CAN CONTAIN UP TO 20 CHARACTERS. */
START:    GET LIST( STRING ) ;
          CHARS = LENGTH( STRING ) ;
          IF (CHARS=1) & (STRING='0') THEN
             GO TO STOP ;

          IF CHARS=5 THEN PUT LIST( STRING ) ;

          GO TO START ;
STOP:     END PRINT5 ;
```

The two IF statements in Example No. 8 could have been
written

```
        IF (LENGTH(STRING)=1) & (STRING='0') THEN GO TO STOP ;
    and
        IF LENGTH(STRING)=5 THEN PUT LIST( STRING ) ;
```

but by using the fixed-point variable CHARS, we avoid computing
the string length more than once.

The number of characters in a string is always an integer,
that is, a string always contains a whole number of characters.
Although this may be obvious, you will find it worthwhile to
remember where integers must appear, and where they may or
may not appear. The result of the LENGTH function is always
an integer.

The PICTURE attribute may be used instead of the
CHARACTER attribute to specify a character string variable.
If PICTURE is used, neither the CHARACTER nor the VARYING
attribute may appear.

The specification characters used to describe character
string variables are:

> A   specifies an alphabetic character, or blank
>
> X   specifies any character

82

The specification character '9' specifies that the corresponding position may contain any decimal digit (as it does when used in a PICTURE for arithmetic variables), or blank.

In order for a PICTURE specification to specify a character string variable, at least one of the specification characters must be 'A' or 'X'.

PICTURE cannot be used to specify a string of varying length.

In addition to character string data, PL/I programs can operate on bit string data. A bit is a single binary digit (0 or 1). A bit string is a sequence of binary digits; the number of digits in the string is the length of the string.

Bit string data, like all other kinds of data in PL/I, can be constant or variable. Bit string constants have the general form

'bit string'B

where bit string is a sequence of binary digits (0's and/or 1's). The "B" following the terminal quote mark specifies that the string is a bit string; if it were omitted, the string would appear to be a character string constant consisting of alphabetic 0's and 1's rather than binary 0's and 1's.

A bit string constant may also be specified as a bit string preceded by a replication factor. The following constants are identical:

'100100100'B

(3)'100'B

Bit string variables must appear in a DECLARE statement with the BIT attribute, e.g.,

DECLARE name BIT (length) ;

where length specifies the length of the string in bits. Note that when a name in a DECLARE statement has the CHARACTER attribute the length specification refers to characters; when it has the BIT attribute, the length specification refers to bits. The CHARACTER and BIT attributes are mutually exclusive.

Bit string variables may also have the VARYING attribute, in which case the length specification states the maximum number of bits which the variable may contain.

The LENGTH function may be used with bit string data, just as with character string data, but it returns the length of the string in bits instead of in characters. The number of bits in a string must always, of course, be an integer.

Bit strings of length 1 are particularly important. Such a string can contain a single binary digit, i.e., a single 1 or a single 0. Thus, a bit string of length 1 can be used to represent a "true" or a "false" condition, i.e., either of the two possible logical values.

The similarity of conditions (Chapter 2) and bit strings of length 1 should be apparent. In fact, when the computer evaluates a condition, the result is a bit string of length 1; this bit string is then tested and the truth or falsity of the original condition is determined by the outcome of the test. Thus, we can substitute a bit string of length 1 for a condition in an IF statement. The general form of such an IF statement is

IF b THEN statement ;

where b is either a condition, as in Chapter 2, or a bit string constant or variable (normally the latter) of length 1. If b is a condition, it is converted to a one-bit string by the computer; if b is a one-bit string originally, it is tested directly.

Whenever a condition is evaluated during execution the outcome is expressed as a bit string of length 1.

A bit string of length 1 has a numeric value of 0 or 1 in addition to its logical value of false or true, respectively. It follows, then, that a one-bit string can be used in either or both logical and arithmetic operations. For example, the statement

$$X = (A>B) + (C=D) ;$$

will assign a value of 0, 1, or 2 to the variable X. Each of the expressions (A>B) and (C=D) will have a logical value of true or false, i.e., 1 or 0. These values, which are also numeric, are added - an arithmetic operation - to give one of the three possible numeric results. The variable X, of course, must be an arithmetic variable or a bit string of length 2 (or more), because it is possible for it to assume a numeric value of two, which requires two bits to represent.

What values can be assigned to X in this statement? (Recall that the symbol | means "or".)

$$X = (A>B) | (C=D) ;$$

Bit string variables of length 1 are sometimes called "Boolean variables" because they always carry one of the two possible logical, or "Boolean" values: true, or false. Similarly, the two bit string constants of length 1 ('1'B and '0'B) are sometimes called "Boolean constants."

The "not" operator (¬) applied to a one-bit string specifies that its value is to be reversed, i.e., subtracted from 1. It does not specify that a positive numeric value is to be made negative (or a negative made positive). "Positive" and "negative" are meaningless in a logical sense; only "true" and "false" have meaning. If a condition is "not true" (¬'1'B), it is "false" ('0'B). Conversely, if a condition is "not false" it is "true."

To summarize, there are two kinds of string data in PL/I: character strings, and bit strings. Character strings are used most frequently to manipulate alphabetic data, while bit strings are used most frequently in logical operations. Bit strings in general are of little interest except in more advanced applications, but one-bit strings have application in even the simplest logical operations.

There is a set of string operators in PL/I which are used to operate directly on character and bit string data. These operators and their uses are discussed in Chapter 10, Character Manipulation.

Label Data

Label data are constants or variables which assume labels as their values. Labels, as you know, are used to name PL/I statements. When it has been necessary in the examples to transfer to a statement labeled name, the appropriate PL/I statement has been of the form GO TO name, i.e., the statement label has appeared explicitly in a GO TO statement. Statement labels which are explicitly specified in places other than their definition are called label constants.

A label variable is an identifier which appears in a DECLARE statement with the LABEL attribute. The LABEL attribute specifies that the associated variable(s) may take on statement labels as values. The general forms of declaration and assignment of labels as values are, respectively

DECLARE name LABEL ;

and

name = label ;

The following program example, which uses label variables, might be used by a national magazine to print a list of those subscribers who live in a particular geographical region. It is assumed that the data for each subscriber consists of three parts:

ZIP code, name, and address; and that the geographical region

in question is defined by a "key" ZIP code.

The program reads a subscriber's ZIP code. If it matches

the "key" ZIP code, then the name and address are printed; if

not, then the name and address are ignored, and the next ZIP

code is read. Each subscriber is processed in the same way.

The program terminates upon reading a ZIP code of 00000, or,

simply, 0.

```
SUBLIST: PROCEDURE OPTIONS (MAIN) ;
            /* EXAMPLE NO. 9
               SUBSET MAILING LIST. */

            DECLARE (KEYZIP, ZIP) FIXED(5),
                    (NAME, ADDRESS) CHARACTER(20) VARYING,
                    SWITCH LABEL ;

            GET LIST( KEYZIP ) ; /* READ KEY ZIP CODE. */
NEWSUB:     GET LIST( ZIP ) ; /* SUBSCRIBER'S ZIP CODE. */
            IF ZIP=0 THEN GO TO FINISH ;
            IF ZIP¬=KEYZIP THEN SWITCH = NEWSUB ;
                         ELSE SWITCH = PRINT ;
            GET LIST( NAME, ADDRESS ) ;

            GO TO SWITCH ;   /* THIS CAUSES A TRANSFER
                                EITHER TO NEWSUB OR TO
                                PRINT, DEPENDING ON LAST
                                ZIP CODE. */

PRINT:      PUT LIST( NAME, ADDRESS, ZIP ) ;
            GO TO NEWSUB ; /* PROCESS NEXT SUBSCRIBER. */
FINISH:     END SUBLIST ;
```

A DECLARE statement can specify those labels which a label variable may assume. The general form of such a specification is

$$\text{DECLARE} \quad \underline{\text{name}} \quad \text{LABEL} \, (\, \underline{L_1}, \, \underline{L_2}, \, \ldots \, \underline{Ln} \,) \, ;$$

where the $\underline{L}$'s are label constants. There are some advantages to specifying the permissible values of label variables. For one, it prevents an inadvertent transfer to an unintended label. For another, the more complete DECLARE statement makes it easier to read and understand the program.

Initialization

All three kinds of data (arithmetic, string, and label) can be set to initial values by means of the INITIAL attribute in DECLARE statements. The general form of a DECLARE statement with the INITIAL attribute is

$$\text{DECLARE} \quad \underline{\text{name}} \quad \underline{\text{attributes}} \quad \text{INITIAL} \, (\, \underline{\text{value}} \,) \, ;$$

where $\underline{\text{attributes}}$ may be any appropriate combination of attributes discussed previously, and value is a constant of the appropriate data type.

The following DECLARE statement is a hypothetical statement used to illustrate the proper use of the INITIAL attribute.

```
DECLARE   A FIXED                 INITIAL ( 0 ),
          B FIXED(5)              INITIAL ( 0 ),
          C BIT(1)                INITIAL ( '1'B ),
          D CHARACTER(10)         INITIAL ( (10)' ' ),
          E LABEL ( LA, LB, LC )  INITIAL ( LB )  ;
```

Note that the variables A and B must be declared separately, even though they are both initialized to the same value,
because the precision attributes differ. They would also have
to be declared separately if any other attributes (including the
initial value) differ.

The INITIAL attribute serves a number of useful functions.
Most importantly, it simplifies initialization; if it is not used,
initialization must be accomplished by assignment statements or
some other means which contribute bulk to programs. Another
advantage is that it enables one to see at a glance the initial
values with which a program is working.

Notes on Chapter 3

When specifying fixed-point arithmetic variables, the
decimal (or binary) point need not lie within the variable. For
example, the statement

91

DECLARE name FIXED DECIMAL (3, 4) ;

specifies that name can assume values in the range 0 to 0.0999 (resolution = 0.0001). As another example,

DECLARE name FIXED DECIMAL (2, -1) ;

specifies that name can assume values in the range 0 to 990 (resolution = 10).

One attribute not discussed in this chapter is the mode attribute, which is of interest to scientific programmers. Arithmetic variables may be declared to be of REAL or COMPLEX mode by inclusion of the appropriate attribute in a DECLARE statement. If the mode is not specified, it is assumed to be REAL.

EXERCISES

3.1   What are the range of values and resolution of each of

the identifiers in this DECLARE statement:

```
DECLARE   A DECIMAL FIXED(5),
          B DECIMAL FLOAT(5),
          C DECIMAL FIXED(5,2),
          D BINARY FIXED(3) ;
```

3.2   What are the attributes of the following constants:

```
123                -3.75
'CAT'              0.03
'''CAUSE'           .03
```

3.3   The IF statements in Examples 8 and 9 (pages 81, 89)

could be transposed within the respective programs

without affecting program operation.   Can you think of

any reason why they were written in the sequence shown?

3.4   What will be the output of the program shown on the

following page?

```
ODD:        PROCEDURE OPTIONS (MAIN) ;

            DECLARE   X BIT(1) INITIAL ( '0'B ),
                      Y FIXED INITIAL ( 0 ),
                  Z LABEL( START, STOP ) INITIAL ( START ) ;

START:      X = ¬X ;
            Y = Y + 1 ;

            IF   X   THEN PUT LIST( Y ) ;
            ELSE PUT LIST( -Y ) ;

            IF   Y=10   THEN Z = STOP ;

            GO TO Z ;

STOP:    END ODD ;
```

CHAPTER 4

ARRAYS (TABLES)

It is frequently convenient to collect a number of simple variables into a list or table and use a single name to refer collectively to the list or table. Lists or tables are called <u>arrays</u> in PL/I.

As an illustration of the use of an array, we might want to make up a list of four kinds of automobiles and refer to the entire list by the identifier CARS. Such a list can be visualized like this:

CARS   (1) | FORD

(2) | CHEVY

(3) | OLDS

(4) | VOLKSWAGEN

In this illustration, CARS is the name of a four-element array. The individual elements are numbered 1, 2, 3, and 4. The contents of each element is a character string representing the name of an automobile. The following program example declares CARS to be a four-element array, and then places the appropriate automobile names into the array.

```
LIST_CARS:   PROCEDURE OPTIONS (MAIN) ;
                /* EXAMPLE NO. 10
                    DECLARE A FOUR-ELEMENT ARRAY AND PLACE
                    NAMES OF AUTOMOBILES IN THE ELEMENTS. */

                DECLARE CARS(4) CHARACTER(10) ;

                CARS(1) = 'FORD' ;
                CARS(2) = 'CHEVY' ;
                CARS(3) = 'OLDS' ;
                CARS(4) = 'VOLKSWAGEN' ;
                PUT LIST (CARS) ;

             END LIST_CARS ;
```

The statement

```
DECLARE CARS(4) CHARACTER(10) ;
```

declares the name CARS to be the name of a four-element array. The entire array, that is, each element of the array, has the CHARACTER attribute and a length attribute of 10. These attributes should be familiar from the preceding chapter.

The 4 in parentheses is called the <u>dimension attribute</u> and means that CARS is the name of a list having a "dimension" or "length" of four.

The general form of an array declaration is

$$\text{DECLARE} \quad \underline{\text{name}} \quad (\underline{\text{dimension}}) \quad \underline{\text{other attributes}} ;$$

where <u>other attributes</u> are as described in the preceding chapter. When an attribute, e.g., FIXED, is applied to an array declaration, it refers to all of the elements in the array. Thus, we can think of an array as a collection of homogeneous information, i.e., data having the same attributes.

The array CARS as declared in Example No. 10 can contain up to four data items. If we needed a longer list, we would have to rewrite the DECLARE statement to increase the dimension attribute. Similarly, if any of the items in the list were to contain more than ten characters, the length specification on the CHARACTER attribute would have to be increased.

The construction DECLARE CARS(4) tells the computer that CARS is the name of a four-element array, but it also tells the computer something else, namely, that the first element of the array has the number 1 and the last has the number 4. These numbers, which identify specific elements, are called <u>subscripts</u>.

Both of the following arrays have four elements. In illustration (a) the elements are referenced by subscript values 1, 2, 3, and 4; in illustration (b) the elements are referenced by subscript values 0, 1, 2, and 3. The corresponding DECLARE

statements are shown above the illustrations.

DECLARE A(4) ;   DECLARE B(0:3) ;

A (1)   B (0)

   (2)   (1)

   (3)   (2)

   (4)   (3)

(a)   (b)

In illustration (a) the subscript 1 refers to the first element

of array A, while in illustration (b) the subscript 1 refers to the

second element of array B. The subscript value which refers to

the first element of an array is called the lower bound; the value

which refers to the last element is called the upper bound. Both

bounds can be specified in a DECLARE statement:

DECLARE name (lower bound : upper bound) ;

If the lower bound (and the colon) are omitted, the lower

bound is assumed to be 1. Thus,

DECLARE name (10) ;

is equivalent to

$$DECLARE \ \underline{name} \ (1{:}10) \ ;$$

The upper bound must be greater than or equal to the lower bound and both bounds must, for the moment, be decimal integer constants. Except for these restrictions, the subscript bounds can be any numbers you care to choose. (Either or both can even be negative).

Suppose the XYZ Company wishes to perform some analysis of sales figures for the years 1963 to 1965, based on the sales data for each of the three years. For this example, assume that the only results desired are 1) total sales, and 2) average sales. The program might look like this:

```
XYZ_3:    PROCEDURE OPTIONS (MAIN) ;
             /* EXAMPLE NO. 11
                XYZ COMPANY, SALES ANALYSIS, 1963-65. */

             DECLARE (SALES(1963:1965), TOTAL, AVG)
                                 DECIMAL FIXED(10,2) ;

             GET LIST(SALES(1963), SALES(1964), SALES(1965)) ;
             TOTAL = SALES(1963) + SALES(1964) + SALES(1965) ;
             AVG = TOTAL/3 ;
             PUT LIST( TOTAL, AVG ) ;
          END XYZ_3 ;
```

The array SALES was declared in the example to have bounds of 1963 and 1965, because these bounds simplify reference to the array. For example, to obtain sales for the year 1963, we refer simply to SALES(1963).

The attributes DECIMAL FIXED(10, 2) as used in Example No. 11 apply to the array SALES as well as to the two simple variables, TOTAL and AVG.

The range of values of subscripts are established by the dimension attribute in DECLARE statements, and subscripts outside this range are meaningless. In Example No. 11, for instance, it would be meaningless to try to reference SALES(1966) because the upper subscript bound on the array SALES is declared to be 1965.

Zero is frequently a very convenient lower bound. For example, when working with a polynomial of the form

$$a_0 + a_1 x + a_2 x^2 + \ldots$$

it is convenient to hold the coefficients, a_i, in an array. (In the notation a_i, i is called a subscript and it is therefore very consistent to place the i'th coefficient in the i'th element of the array.)

An individual array element has precisely the same properties as a simple variable. It can be assigned a value, e.g., SALES(1963) could have appeared to the left of an assignment operator in Example No. 11; and it can have only one value at a time. In order to use an array element as a variable, however, the subscript must be specified. Individual array elements are thus called subscripted variables.

The subscript(s) used in an array declaration must, for the moment, be decimal integer constants, but the subscripts used to reference elements of arrays may be any expressions which have values within the specified subscript range. The process of referencing elements of arrays is called indexing, and the constant, variable, or other expression used as a subscript is sometimes called the index. In Example No. 12, below, the variable I is used as an index.

```
POW2: PROCEDURE OPTIONS (MAIN) ;
          /* EXAMPLE NO. 12
             FILL AN ARRAY WITH POWERS OF TWO, SUCH THAT
             A(0)=2**0, A(1)=2**1, ... */

          DECLARE ( A(0:10), I ) FIXED INITIAL(1) ;

LOOP:     A(I) = A(I-1) + A(I-1) ;
          PUT LIST (A(I)) ;
          I = I + 1 ;
          IF I<=10 THEN GO TO LOOP ;

          END POW2 ;
```

101

The initial value of array elements can be specified by the INITIAL attribute. In the case of arrays, the INITIAL attribute can specify a number of initial values to initialize a corresponding number of array elements. The first element in the array (the element having the lowest subscript) is set to the first initial value, the second is set to the second initial value, etc., until the list of initial values is exhausted. The statement

DECLARE A(10) FIXED INITIAL (0, -5, 3) ;

would set the first three elements of A to 0, -5, and 3, respectively; the values of the next seven elements of A are said to be undefined. *

In Example No. 12, only one initial value is specified. This value is placed in the first element of the array A, i.e., A(0). The INITIAL attribute, since it contains only one initial value, is also applicable to the simple variable, I, used in the program. Had it been necessary to initialize more than one element of A, it would have been necessary to declare the array and the variable separately and use an appropriate INITIAL attribute in each case.

---

* Unless explicitly specified by the INITIAL attribute or a GET or assignment statement, you should never assume that an array element or a simple variable has a particular value.

Another way to specify a list of initial values for an array

is replication. The statement

```
DECLARE A(0:10) INITIAL ( (11)0 ) ;
```

specifies that the entire array A is to be initialized to 0. (Note

that A has eleven elements.)

What are the subscript bounds, number of elements, and

initial values in each of these arrays?

```
DECLARE   A(5),
          B(-3:3) INITIAL( (3)-1 ),
          C(10) INITIAL( (2)1, (3)2 ) ;
```

Answers: (? = "undefined")

	bounds	# elements	values
A	1, 5	5	?, ?, ?, ?, ?
B	-3, 3	7	-1, -1, -1, ?, ?, ?, ?
C	1, 10	10	1, 1, 2, 2, 2, ?, ?, ?, ?, ?

Arrays can be organized in various ways to make them

most convenient to use. In Example No. 11, page 99, the subscripts were chosen to reflect the various years in question; to refer to sales in the year 1965, we referred to SALES(1965). In this case, the choice of subscripts helped to make the array most convenient to use.

Suppose now, we want to represent a checkerboard in the computer. We could do this by declaring an array of 64 elements, each element corresponding to one of the squares on the checkerboard, but it would be much more convenient to visualize the array like this:

	1	2	3	4	5	6	7	8
1	1,1	1,2						
2	2,1							
3								
4								
5								
6								
7								7,8
8							8,7	8,8

Each element of the board has two indices: the first specifies the row, and the second specifies the column. Conceptually,
the checkerboard is not a list of 64 elements; instead, it is a
square, having two dimensions ("horizontal" and "vertical"). It
has eight squares in each dimension.

What we must do now is specify to the compiler by means
of a DECLARE statement that we want to think of this array as an
8 by 8 matrix; not as a list of 64 elements. The appropriate
DECLARE statement is

```
DECLARE   CHECKERBOARD(8,8) ;
```

This DECLARE statement declares a two-dimensional
array; the upper subscript bounds for each dimension are separated by a comma. (The lower bounds are 1 in each dimension.)
The first dimension indicates the number of rows; the second
indicates the number of columns.

Lower, as well as upper bounds may be specified for
either or both dimensions. The DECLARE statements at the
top of the next page are all equivalent.

```
DECLARE CHECKERBOARD( 8,8 ) ;
DECLARE CHECKERBOARD( 1:8,8 ) ;
DECLARE CHECKERBOARD( 8,1:8 ) ;
DECLARE CHECKERBOARD( 1:8,1:8 ) ;
```

Arrays in PL/I may have any number of dimensions. Although the arrays used so far in this chapter have had physical representations (a list, a checkerboard), there are no such representations for arrays of more than three dimensions. Nevertheless, n-dimensional arrays do have their uses. A four-dimensional array might be used, for example, to maintain a directory of individuals in an office which has four-digit telephone extension numbers. The program example on the following page will read four digits representing a telephone extension and print the name of the individual to whom that extension is assigned. (We ignore the means by which the data would have been placed in the array originally; the purpose of the program is to illustrate n-dimensional indexing.)

The number of subscripts (indices) used in a subscripted name must always be the same as the number of dimensions declared for the name.

```
DIRECTORY:  PROCEDURE OPTIONS (MAIN) ;
            /* EXAMPLE NO. 13
               READ FOUR DIGITS CORRESPONDING TO A
               TELEPHONE EXTENSION AND PRINT THE NAME
               OF THE INDIVIDUAL ON THAT EXTENSION. */

            DECLARE NAME(9,0:9,0:9,0:9) CHARACTER(20),
                    (D1, D2, D3, D4) FIXED ;
            GET LIST(D1, D2, D3, D4) ;
            PUT LIST( NAME(D1,D2,D3,D4) ) ;
            END DIRECTORY ;
```

Array names, without subscripts, may under certain conditions be used to form array expressions. If A is the name of an array, then the expression 2*A means that the value in each element of A is to be doubled. If we want to assign the values obtained to another array, B, we could write

$$B = 2*A ;$$

provided that B has the same number of dimensions and the same subscript bounds as A. If both arrays have three elements, then the above assignment statement is equivalent to

$$B(1) = 2*A(1) ; B(2) = 2*A(2) ; B(3) = 2*A(3) ;$$

Arrays having the same number of dimensions and the

same subscript bounds, i.e., arrays which are identical except for their names, can be used in the same way as simple variables. Array operations are performed element by element, so the statement

$$A = A + 1 ;$$

using array A as an operand is identical to the following sequence of statements which use simple variables as operands.

$$A(1) = A(1) + 1 ;$$
$$A(2) = A(2) + 1 ;$$
$$\bullet$$
$$\bullet$$

The following program places the largest number from each corresponding position of two arrays into a third array:

```
MAX:   PROCEDURE OPTIONS (MAIN) ;
          /* EXAMPLE NO. 14
             ILLUSTRATE ARRAY EXPRESSIONS. */

          DECLARE (A(5), B(5), LARGE(5) ) FIXED ;

          GET LIST(A, B) ;
          LARGE = A + (B>A)*(B-A) ;
          PUT LIST( LARGE ) ;
       END MAX ;
```

This table shows values are computed for the array
LARGE in Example No. 14, assuming the arrays A and B
contain the indicated values:

	A	B	LARGE = A + (B>A)*(B-A)
(1)	1	-1	1 + (0) * (-2) = 1
(2)	2	1	2 + (0) * (-1) = 2
(3)	3	3	3 + (0) * (0) = 3
(4)	4	5	4 + (1) * (5-4) = 5
(5)	5	7	5 + (1) * (7-5) = 7

Multi-dimensional array operations are performed in
"row major" order, which means that the rightmost subscript
is varied most rapidly and the leftmost subscript is varied
least rapidly. The following examples illustrate row major
order in the three contexts where it is most important.

Initialization:

```
DECLARE A(2,3) FIXED INITIAL ( 1, 2, 3, 4, 5, 6 ) ;
```

places the following values in A:

$$A(1, 1) = 1 \qquad A(1, 2) = 2 \qquad A(1, 3) = 3$$

$$A(2, 1) = 4 \qquad A(2, 2) = 5 \qquad A(2, 3) = 6$$

Input/Output:

```
DECLARE B(2,3) FIXED INITIAL ( 1, 2, 3, 4, 5, 6 ) ;
PUT LIST( B ) ;
```

causes the following sequence of numbers to be printed:

1 2 3 4 5 6

Array Expressions:

```
DECLARE C(2,2) FIXED INITIAL ( 1, 2, 3, 4 ) ;
C = C + C(2,1) ;
```

places the following values in C:

$$C(1, 1) = 4 \qquad C(1, 2) = \ 5$$

$$C(2, 1) = 6 \qquad C(2, 2) = 10$$

(Note that the value of C(2, 1) is modified during execution of the array assignment statement.)

The principle of row major order applies to arrays of any number of dimensions; two-dimensional arrays were used in the preceding examples only to illustrate the principle. How would initial values be assigned to the array declared in this statement?

```
DECLARE A(2,3,4) FIXED INITIAL ( (12)1, (12)2 ) ;
```

So far, we have used arrays to hold two of the three data types (arithmetic and string) described in Chapter 3. Arrays can also contain label data. The following two programs illustrate label arrays and show two different ways in which the contents of their elements can be established. The operation is the same in both cases: read a decimal digit which must be 1, 2, or 3. If 1, read the next ten numbers into array A; if 2, read them into array B; if 3, end the program.

```
FILL_ARRAY: PROCEDURE OPTIONS (MAIN) ;
                DECLARE ( A, B )(10) FLOAT,
                        NUM BINARY FIXED,
                        LAB(3) LABEL INITIAL ( L1, L2, L3 ) ;
START:          GET LIST( NUM ) ;
                GO TO LAB( NUM ) ;
L1:             GET LIST( A ) ; GO TO START ;
L2:             GET LIST( B ) ; GO TO START ;
L3:         END FILL_ARRAY ;
```

```
FILL_ARRAY: PROCEDURE OPTIONS (MAIN) ;

                    DECLARE ( A, B )(10) FLOAT,
                            NUM BINARY FIXED,
                            LAB(3) LABEL ;

START:              GET LIST( NUM ) ;

                    GO TO LAB( NUM ) ;

LAB(1):             GET LIST( A ) ; GO TO START ;
LAB(2):             GET LIST( B ) ; GO TO START ;
LAB(3):         END FILL_ARRAY ;
```

In the solution immediately above, the array LAB contains label constants. LAB(1), for instance, is defined by use to appear at one particular place in the program; LAB(1) always refers to the associated GET statement. In the first solution (on the preceding page), the array LAB contains label variables; the values of its elements could be changed by assignment statements in the program in addition to (or instead of) the initial values established by means of the INITIAL attribute used in the example.

Label arrays provide a very powerful means of controlling program execution. As you write more programs you will find many places where they can be used to simplify program logic and reduce the amount of writing necessary to implement it.

One of the most useful features of arrays is that they simplify the management of large quantities of data. For example,
if a program is to add a thousand numbers, these numbers
could be placed into an array of a thousand elements, and the
required addition could be specified very simply in PL/I:

```
            DECLARE A(1000) FLOAT,
                    I BINARY FIXED INITIAL( 1 ),
                    TOTAL FLOAT INITIAL( 0 ) ;
              .
              .
              .
    LOOP:   TOTAL = TOTAL + A(I) ;
            I = I + 1 ;
            IF  I<=1000   THEN GO TO LOOP ;
              .
              .
              .
```

The basic program structure illustrated above is called
a loop. Program execution proceeds around the loop, each
time adding the contents of the I'th element of the array A to
the accumulating sum (TOTAL). Each time through the loop
the variable I, used as a subscript, has a different value.
After the loop has been executed 1000 times, the variable I
will have the value 1001; the condition in the IF statement will
be false, and execution will proceed in sequence. The important thing to note is that it is necessary to write only three PL/I

113

statements in order to add 1000 numbers. Of course, 1000 is an arbitrary figure; the limit could have been as large or as small as appropriate; the process would still require only three statements.

The concept of loops is fundamental to data processing, and is practically essential to efficient use of the computer. We have been using loops in almost all of our examples for one purpose or another. Every time we say "GO TO START" we are really implementing a loop.

Chapter 2 showed how the DO statement could be used to group a number of statements together into a logical entity called a DO group. The DO statement can also be used to specify that the statements between the DO and the corresponding END are to be executed repeatedly. This kind of specification is called a DO loop, and here is how a DO loop might be used to add 1000 numbers:

```
DECLARE A(1000) FLOAT,
        I BINARY FIXED,
        TOTAL FLOAT INITIAL( 0 ) ;
  .
  .
  .
DO I = 1 BY 1 TO 1000 ;
    TOTAL = TOTAL + A(I) ;
END ;
  .
  .
  .
```

114

The form of the DO statement used in the preceding example specifies that the statements between the DO and the END (a single statement in the example) are to be executed for each value of the variable I from 1 to 1000 in steps of 1. The variable is first set to 1 and the statement is executed. The variable is then "stepped up" by 1 because the DO statement specifies BY 1, and then, assuming the variable is not greater than 1000, the statement is executed again. The process continues until the variable is greater than the limit, at which time execution proceeds to the first statement following the END statement for the loop. A flow chart of the process is included at the end of this chapter.

A recommended practice is to label the DO statement and use that label on the corresponding END statement. This practice, together with indentation, will help to clarify programs and make them easier to read. The program example on the following page illustrates the practice. The program uses the built-in function SIN to compute and print a table of the trigonometric sine function for angles from 0 to 2π radians in steps of 0.1 radian. The limit of 6.28 used in the program is the value of 2π ($\pi = 3.14159...$) to an accuracy within the step size of 0.1.

```
SINE: PROCEDURE OPTIONS (MAIN) ;
         /* EXAMPLE NO. 15
            PRINT TABLE OF SINES. */

         DECLARE X FLOAT ;

LOOP:    DO X = 0 BY 0.1 TO 6.28 ;
            PUT LIST( X, SIN(X) ) ;
         END LOOP ;
      END SINE ;
```

DO loops have the general form

DO <u>control variable</u> = <u>specifications</u> ;

<u>statement(s)</u> ;

END ;

where <u>control variable</u> is a simple or subscripted variable, and
<u>specifications</u> specify the various values which the control vari-
able is to assume. The specifications may take several forms:

(a)   <u>expression</u>$_1$, <u>expression</u>$_2$, ... <u>expression</u>$_n$

specifies that the statement(s) in the DO

loop are to be executed, first with the

control variable set to the value of

116

expression$_1$, again with the control vari-

able set to the value of expression$_2$, etc.

(b)   expression$_1$ BY expression$_2$ TO expression$_3$

specifies that the statement(s) in the DO

loop are to be executed with the control

variable set to the value of expression$_1$

and increased by the value of expression$_2$

at the start of each subsequent pass

through the loop, until the value of the

control variable exceeds the value of

expression$_3$. (If the value of expression$_2$

is negative, the control variable is

decremented at the start of each sub-

sequent pass through the loop until its

value is less than the value of expression$_3$.)

This form of specification may also be

written

expression$_1$ TO expression$_3$ BY expression$_2$

(c)   WHILE (<u>condition</u>)

> specifies that the statement(s) in the DO
>
> loop are to be executed repeatedly as long
>
> as <u>condition</u> is true. <u>Condition</u> is evalu-
>
> ated prior to each pass through the loop.

In principle, any looping operation can be specified by any of these three forms of DO specifications. The one you should use for a particular purpose is the one which is most convenient for the purpose. Each of the following DO loops sets the first ten elements of the array X to zero:

```
A:      DO I = 1, 2, 3, 4, 5, 6, 7, 8, 9, 10 ;
           X(I) = 0 ;
        END A ;

B:      DO I = 1 BY 1 TO 10 ;
           X(I) = 0 ;
        END B ;

        I = 1 ;
C:      DO WHILE ( I<=10 ) ;
           X(I) = 0 ;
           I = I + 1 ;
        END C ;
```

The labels on the three preceding DO statements correspond to the three forms of DO specifications. For this particular application, form B is the simplest. Form C requires the
use of two additional assignment statements.

Forms B and C can be combined into a single specification:

```
BC:    DO I = 1 BY 1 WHILE ( I<=10 ) ;
          X(I) = 0 ;
       END BC ;
```

which simplifies the construction somewhat. Still, for this application, form B is the simplest.*

DO loops have the following characteristics:

1. The specifications may consist of any expressions; they need not contain only decimal integer constants.

2. The expressions in the specifications are evaluated only once, at the time the DO statement is first encountered. Thus, the expression values cannot be effectively modified by statements within the loop. However, the control variable can be modified; if such modifications give it a value outside the specified range, the loop will not be repeated after the current pass is completed.

3. A GO TO statement within the scope of a DO loop may transfer control to a point outside the loop, thus terminating the loop prematurely.

4. A GO TO statement outside a DO loop must not transfer to a point within the loop. (A GO TO statement may, however, transfer to a point within a DO group.)

---

* The DO loops used for illustration set the first ten elements of array X to zero. If the array contains only ten elements, then of course the simplest way to set all of the elements to zero is the array assignment statement X = 0 ;

5.   The value of the control variable after control has left a DO loop depends on the conditions under which the loop was left. The following two rules are illustrated by Example No. 16, which follows:

If the loop is terminated normally, the control variable has the first value which fails to meet the conditions for execution of the loop.

If the loop is terminated prematurely, e.g., by a GO TO statement which transfers out of the loop, the value of the control variable is the value it had when the GO TO statement was executed.

```
FIND3:      PROCEDURE OPTIONS (MAIN) ;
            /* EXAMPLE NO. 16
               READ 20 NUMBERS INTO AN ARRAY AND PRINT
               THE LOCATION IN THE LIST OF THE FIRST '3'.
               IF NONE OF THE ELEMENTS CONTAINS '3' THE
               ''LOCATION'' PRINTED WILL BE 21. */

            DECLARE (A(20), I) FIXED ;

            GET LIST( A ) ;
L1:         DO I = 1 BY 1 TO 20 ;
               IF A(I)=3 THEN GO TO L2 ;
            END L1 ;

L2:         PUT LIST( I ) ;

            END FIND3 ;
```

DO loops may be nested. That is, any of the statements in a DO loop may themselves be DO statements. In Example No. 17 on the following page, the loop initiated by the DO statement at L2 is an "inner" loop, nested within the loop initiated by the DO statement at L1. What values will be printed by the program?

```
DO_LOOPS:      PROCEDURE OPTIONS (MAIN) ;

               /* EXAMPLE NO. 17
                  ILLUSTRATE NESTED LOOPS */

               DECLARE (I, J, N1, N2) FIXED INITIAL(0) ;
L1:            DO I = 1 BY 1 TO 10 ;
                  N1 = N1 + 1 ;
L2:               DO J = 1 BY 1 TO 10 ;
                     N2 = N2 + 1 ;
                  END L2 ;
               END L1 ;

               PUT LIST(N1, N2) ;

            END DO_LOOPS ;
```

The answers are, N1 = 10 and N2 = 100. In other words, the assignment statement in the inner loop is executed 100 times; the assignment statement in the outer loop only ten times. Of course, any other statements in the inner loop, had there been any, would also have been executed 100 times, while any other statements in the outer loop would have been executed only ten times. This observation points to a fact which is essential to efficient use of a computer:

> When using nested loops, perform as much computation as possible in the outer loops; perform as little as possible in the innermost loop.

The following two examples illustrate the importance of the

rule. Both programs perform the same operation: summing the

values in a one-dimensional and a two-dimensional array.

```
WRONG:     PROCEDURE OPTIONS (MAIN) ;
           /* EXAMPLE NO. 18
              INEFFICIENT USE OF DO LOOPS. */

           DECLARE (A(10), B(10,10), I, J, SUM1, SUM2)
                                   FIXED ;

           GET LIST (A, B) ;

           SUM1, SUM2 = 0 ;
L1:        DO I = 1 BY 1 TO 10 ;
L2:           DO J = 1 BY 1 TO 10 ;
S1:              SUM1 = SUM1 + A(I) ;
S2:              SUM2 = SUM2 + B(I,J) ;
              END L2 ;
           END L1 ;

           PUT LIST (SUM1, SUM2) ;

           END WRONG ;
```

```
RIGHT:     PROCEDURE OPTIONS (MAIN) ;
           /* EXAMPLE NO. 19
              EFFICIENT USE OF DO LOOPS. */

           DECLARE (A(10), B(10,10), I, J, SUM1, SUM2)
                                   FIXED ;

           GET LIST (A, B) ;

           SUM1, SUM2 = 0 ;
L1:        DO I = 1 BY 1 TO 10 ;
S1:           SUM1 = SUM1 + A(I) ;
L2:           DO J = 1 BY 1 TO 10 ;
S2:              SUM2 = SUM2 + B(I,J) ;
              END L2 ;
           END L1 ;

           PUT LIST (SUM1, SUM2) ;

           END RIGHT ;
```

122

In WRONG (Example No. 18) the statements at S1 and S2 will each be executed 100 times, for a total of 200 statement executions. Moving statement S1 into the outer loop (because it doesn't have to be in the inner loop), as in RIGHT (Example No. 19), S2 will be executed 100 times, as before, but S1 will be executed only 10 times, for a total of 110 statement executions. Merely by moving a single statement from an inner loop to an outer loop, we have cut the computer time required to solve the problem almost in half!

The END statement corresponding to an inner DO state-ment must appear prior to the END statement corresponding to the next outer DO statement. The required construction is illus-trated schematically below, where each vertical line indicates the scope of a DO statement.

(a) – correct   (b) – incorrect

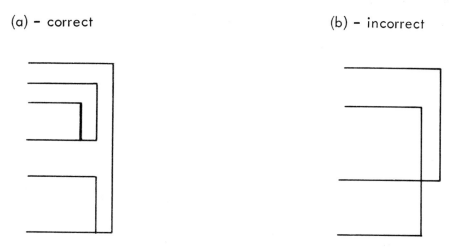

If labels are not used following END statements, the compiler will interpret each END statement as corresponding to the last DO statement for which an END statement has not yet been provided.

If labels are used following END statements, a practice which is highly recommended, then the compiler will interpret each END statement as corresponding to the DO statement having the same label <u>as well as all DO statements within its scope.</u> To illustrate, the following statement will sum the elements of a three-dimensional array:

```
        SUM = 0 ;
L1:     DO I = 1 BY 1 TO 10 ;
            DO J = 1 BY 1 TO 10 ;
                DO K = 1 BY 1 TO 10 ;
                    SUM = SUM + A(I,J,K) ;
        END L1 ;
```

The END statement terminates all three DO loops because the label, L1, matches the label on the outermost DO statement.

To summarize, this chapter has introduced arrays as collections of data and has shown some of the ways in which arrays can be used to simplify management of data. The DO statement is a very simple but powerful means of specifying iteration, which is one of the things a computer does best. The DO loop has been introduced here predominantly as a device for manipulation of data in arrays, but it is by no means limited to applications of this kind. (See Example No. 15, for example.)

Notes on Chapter 4

1. The expression A*B where A and B are arrays, does not represent matrix multiplication. Instead, it specifies that corresponding elements of A and B are to be multiplied.

2. PL/I contains several built-in functions which are useful when working with arrays. Two of these are SUM and PROD, which can be used to sum and multiply all the data in an array, respectively. This statement would perform the same function as the loop shown on page 113:

```
TOTAL = SUM( A ) ;
```

3. Another built-in function, MAX, has the value of the largest of its arguments (there must be two or more arguments). This statement could be used to simplify program Example

No. 14, page 108:

```
LARGE = MAX( A, B ) ;
```

4.   A DO statement of the form

        DO <u>control variable</u> = <u>expression</u>$_1$ BY <u>expression</u>$_2$

                        TO <u>expression</u>$_3$

                        WHILE(<u>condition</u>) ;

          <u>statement(s)</u> ;

       END ;

can be represented by the flow chart on the following page, assuming that <u>expression</u>$_2$ is positive. If it is not, the loop is terminated when <u>control variable</u><<u>expression</u>$_3$.

5.   BY may be omitted from a DO specification, in which case the step expression (<u>expression</u>$_2$ in the notation used here) is assumed to be 1. These statements are equivalent:

```
DO V = A BY 1 TO B ;
DO V = A TO B ;
```

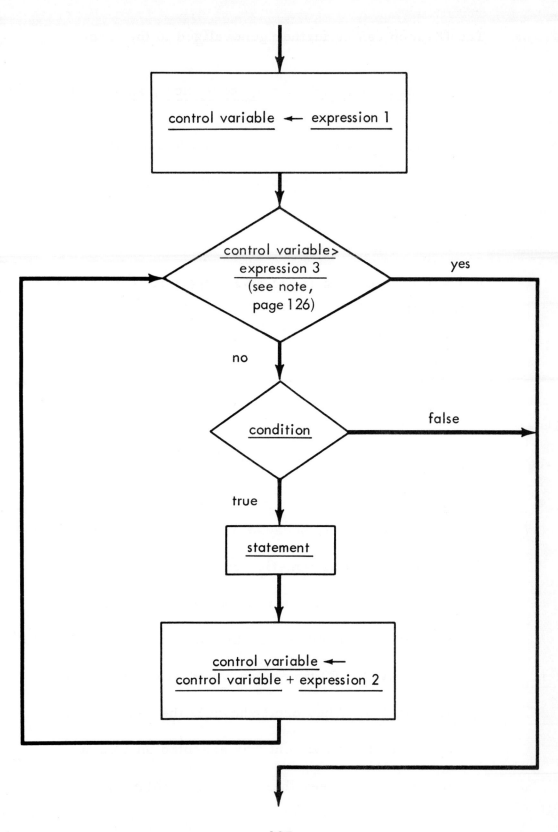

6.   The DO loop can be further generalized to the form

$$DO \quad \underline{\text{control variable}} \; = \; \underline{\text{specification}_1}, \; \underline{\text{specification}_2}, \; \ldots$$

where each specification is one of the forms shown on pages 116-119. For example, the PUT statement in the DO loop

```
DO I = 1, 2, 5 BY 1 TO 10, 12 BY 2 WHILE ( I<=16 ), 3, 4 ;
   PUT LIST( I ) ;
END ;
```

will print each value of the variable I, namely,

    1, 2, 5, 6, 7, 8, 9, 10, 12, 14, 16, 3, and 4.

7.   Chapter 1 stated that, because most computers do not use decimal (base ten) arithmetic, certain common decimal fractions cannot always be represented accurately. The following DO statement causes the decimal fraction 0.01 to be added to itself 100 times; we would expect the final result to be 1.0. The result shown is the result actually obtained when the statement was executed on a computer which uses base sixteen (hexadecimal) arithmetic.

```
DECLARE I FIXED,
        SUM FLOAT INITIAL ( 0 ) ;

DO I = 1 TO 100 ;
    SUM = SUM + 0.01 ;
END ;
PUT LIST( SUM ) ;
```

The result, exactly as produced by the computer, is:

9.99999E-01   (i.e., 0.999999)

This example illustrates the characteristic of <u>roundoff</u>
<u>error</u>, which is present in some degree in almost every
arithmetic operation involving decimal fractions. Uncon-
trolled, as it is in this example, the error can be com-
pounded and the final results of the computation may be
grossly inaccurate.

There is no general remedy for problems due to
roundoff, but two simple ways to minimize it are:

1. Increase the precision attribute of the operands.
    (This may reduce the speed of computation.)

2. Perform operations in a certain sequence in

order to maintain accuracy when evaluating expressions. Although this usually requires prior knowledge of the values of the operands, a good general principle is to try to form expressions that do not contain decimal fractions. For example, 10*A will probably give a more accurate result than A/0.1; A/10 may be more accurate than 0.1*A.

It is important to note that the number of digits printed by a particular computer is not necessarily an indication of accuracy, i.e., answers printed to ten decimal places are not necessarily more accurate than answers printed to five decimal places.

EXERCISES

4.1   How many elements are there in the array used in

Example No. 13 (page 107)?

4.2   Aside from being inefficient, Example No. 18 (page 122)

will not produce the correct results (as defined at the top

of page 122). If the program were executed, could the

correct results be deduced from the erroneous results

printed by the computer?

4.3   Write a PL/I program which reads 20 fixed-point decimal

numbers (precision 5,2) into an array and then prints the

largest value in the array.

4.4   A, B, and C are two-dimensional arrays of 15 elements in

each dimension. Write a PL/I program to form the matrix

product AxB in C.

Matrix multiplication in the context of this exercise means

that each element of C must take on the value

$$C(I, J) = A(I, 1)*B(1, J) + A(I, 2)*B(2, J) + \ldots A(I, 15)*B(15, J)$$

4.5 Write a PL/I program which does the following: reads a string of 15 alphabetic characters into an array (one character per element). Finds each occurrence of the letter Q, and forms a list (using another array) of the positions in which it appears. Use the first element of the list to count the number of appearances of the letter Q.

For example, if the input data were the string

ACGQXY PQRMLAZQT

the constructed list would contain

3, 4, 8, 14 (Q appears 3 times, in positions 4, 8, and 14)

4.6 Generalize the program written for Exercise 4.5 so that it will read a single "key" character prior to reading the 15 characters; and forms the list based on the key character.

4.7 Read ten numbers into a one-dimensional array and place them in ascending sequence, i.e., sort them into ascending order. Print the resulting list. Re-sort the numbers into descending sequence, i.e., reverse the array, and print

the resulting list. Use only one array.

4.8   Use a DO loop to evaluate the expression

$$\frac{X}{X^2 - 1}$$

for values of X from -3 to +3 in steps of 0.5. Allow for

the possibility that some values of X in this range may

cause division by zero; do not evaluate the expression

for these values. Instead, print the message

'CAUSES DIVISION BY ZERO'

For all other values of X, print X and the resulting value

of the expression.

CHAPTER 5

STRUCTURES

Arrays, as shown in Chapter 4, are collections or aggregates of homogeneous data. In many cases you will find it convenient or necessary not only to collect data, but to collect data in some prescribed way; and the data may or may not be homogeneous. For example, in preparing a payroll, there may be several items of information pertaining to each individual employee. These items would include his name (characters), employee number, hours worked, etc. In other words, it would be convenient to group certain items of information under each employee's name: each employee will have his own number, rate of pay, etc. The information pertaining to each employee is non-homogeneous - his name is a character string, but the rest of the information is arithmetic - so the information cannot be organized into an array.

Non-homogeneous and/or logically related data can be organized as a structure in PL/I. The essential difference between a structure and an array is that an array is simply an

aggregation of data while a structure is a hierarchical collection

of data. Another difference is that an array may contain only

homogeneous data, while a structure may or may not contain

homogeneous data.

A structure in PL/I can be likened to an outline for a book.

The material to be included in the book is divided into parts, and

the individual parts may be further subdivided. A typical outline

might have the form

    I.

            A.

                    1.

                    2.

            B.

    II.

            A.

            B.

where the various levels are denoted by Roman numerals,

capital letters, Arabic numerals, etc. Levels which are not

further subdivided are called elementary levels.

There are three differences between PL/I structures and outlines:

1. All levels in structures are denoted by numbers.

2. Levels need not be divided into at least two parts, as they must be in an outline.

3. Only the elementary levels in a structure can contain data, while a subdivided level in an outline might correspond to a few general remarks in the text prior to treating the elemental subjects.

In a payroll program, the information pertaining to each employee might be organized as a structure. We could view such a structure as

    1   EMPLOYEE

        2 NAME

        2 NUMBER

        2 HOURS_WORKED

        2 RATE_OF_PAY

        etc.

The number to the left of each identifier is a level number. Within this structure each item with the number 2 is of the same hierarchy; all are subordinate to the item with the number 1.

136

The preceding structure contains four elementary levels:

NAME, NUMBER, HOURS_WORKED, and RATE_OF_PAY.

Thus, the structure contains four data items.

It might be convenient to break some of the data down

further. For example, it might be desirable to distinguish

between straight time and overtime hours worked. We might

then visualize the structure as

```
        1    EMPLOYEE

             2  NAME

             2  NUMBER

             2  HOURS_WORKED

                  3   STRAIGHT_TIME

                  3   OVERTIME

             2  RATE_OF_PAY
```

The structure now contains five elementary levels. The

name HOURS_WORKED is no longer an elementary level; it is

an identifier which refers collectively to the two data items

STRAIGHT_TIME and OVERTIME, which are elementary levels.

In principle, we can subdivide a structure into as many

levels as we need. In PL/I, a structure must have one and only one level 1. The name given to this level (EMPLOYEE in the preceding representations) is the name of the entire structure.

The structure on the preceding page would be implemented in PL/I by the statement

```
DECLARE   1 EMPLOYEE,
          2 NAME CHARACTER(20),
          2 NUMBER FIXED,
          2 HOURS_WORKED,
          (3 STRAIGHT_TIME,
           3 OVERTIME) FIXED,
          2 RATE_OF_PAY  FIXED ;
```

The indentation used in the above statement is, of course, arbitrary. It is good practice to indent in order to emphasize the data organization being declared.

The DECLARE statement above is very similar to the structure representation on the preceding page. There are only two differences: attributes have been included in the DECLARE statement, and each level name is separated from the subsequent level number by a comma. Parentheses are used to factor the FIXED attribute, which applies to the elementary levels NUMBER, STRAIGHT_TIME, OVERTIME; and RATE_OF_PAY.

Attributes may be applied only to elementary levels,
because these are the only levels which contain data.

As a rule, data for any application can be organized into a
structure. For example, a program to solve quadratic equations
involves five data items: three coefficients, and two roots.
These items could be organized into a structure:

```
DECLARE   1 QUADFUN,
          (2 INPUT_1,
           2 INPUT_2,
           2 INPUT_3,
           2 ROOT_1,
           2 ROOT_2) FLOAT ;
```

This DECLARE statement is rather bulky. It can be
simplified considerably by combining the three input items and
the two roots into two arrays within the structure QUADFUN.
This is accomplished simply by giving a dimension attribute to
the items:

```
DECLARE   1 QUADFUN,
          (2 INPUT(3),
           2 ROOT(2) )  FLOAT ;
```

Now, we have specified the various identifiers to have the
following meanings:

QUADFUN is the name of a hierarchical collection
of five data items: three input values and two root
values.

INPUT is the name of an array containing three
data items. Individual items are referenced as
usual, i.e., INPUT(1), INPUT(2), and INPUT(3).
The identifier INPUT by itself, of course, refers
to all three items.

ROOT is the name of an array containing two
data items.

Suppose we wanted to organize the data for ten equations,
rather than just one. The data for each of the ten equations
would consist of five items. The simplest way to declare ten
such sets of data is merely to dimension the structure QUADFUN:

```
DECLARE   1 QUADFUN(10),
          (2 INPUT(3),
           2 ROOT(2) )   FLOAT ;
```

The above statement allocates space for 50 data items in
the computer, 10 sets of 5 items each. The organization of the

140

items can be visualized as

QUADFUN(1)	INPUT(1)	element	1 in the computer
	INPUT(2)		2
	INPUT(3)		3
	ROOT(1)		4
	ROOT(2)		5
QUADFUN(2)	INPUT(1)		6
	INPUT(2)		7
	INPUT(3)		8
	ROOT(1)		9
	ROOT(2)		10
QUADFUN(3)	INPUT(1)		11
	.		.
	.		.
	.		.
	.		.

Now, among other things, the construction INPUT(1) refers not to a single item, but to <u>ten</u> items. There is an INPUT(1) in each of the ten elements of QUADFUN. In order to refer to a particular INPUT(1), we must <u>qualify</u> the name by the appropriate element of QUADFUN. That is, we must specify a particular element of QUADFUN in conjunction with INPUT(1) in order to refer to a specific INPUT(1).

Qualification in PL/I is specified by a decimal point. To refer to the data in INPUT(1) within QUADFUN(1) we would write

QUADFUN(1).INPUT(1)

which qualifies the "minor" name INPUT(1) by the "major" name QUADFUN(1).

How many data items are referenced by each of these names?

QUADFUN(1)	Answer:	5
QUADFUN(1).INPUT		3
ROOT		20

Qualification is in general required in order to make an identifier unique, i.e., to eliminate any ambiguities in referencing it. In the preceding case, qualification was required because the structure was dimensioned. Another case in which qualification is required occurs when a minor structure has the same name as a minor structure within a different major structure. For example, a program used by a manufacturer might contain three structures:

```
DECLARE  1 PRODUCT_A,
           2 AMOUNT,
           (3 JANUARY,
            3 JULY) FLOAT,

         1 PRODUCT_B,
           2 AMOUNT,
           (3 JANUARY,
            3 JULY) FLOAT,

         1 PRODUCT_C,
           2 AMOUNT,
           (3 JANUARY,
            3 APRIL,
            3 JULY,
            3 OCTOBER) FLOAT ;
```

The identifiers APRIL and OCTOBER are unique; references to them need not be qualified. The identifier JANUARY,
however, is not unique, and so references to JANUARY must be
qualified by the name of the appropriate structure, e.g.,
PRODUCT_A.JANUARY . The <u>fully qualified</u> name is

PRODUCT_A.AMOUNT.JANUARY

which may be used, but which is unnecessary because only
partial qualification is needed to refer to a specific JANUARY .

The qualified name AMOUNT.JANUARY would be ambig-
uous because AMOUNT.JANUARY appears in more than one
structure.

Structures which are identical except, perhaps for the names of various levels, may be used in structure expressions. Two structures are identical when there is a one-to-one correspondence between the elements of the structures.

In a program using the three structures shown on page 143, the statement

PRODUCT_A = PRODUCT_B ;

would be legal, but the statement

PRODUCT_A = PRODUCT_C ;

would not, because PRODUCT_A and PRODUCT_C are not identical structures: they do not contain the same number of elements. However, by using qualified names, we can move individual data items from PRODUCT_C to PRODUCT_A. For example,

PRODUCT_A.JANUARY = PRODUCT_C.APRIL ;

is a legal statement.

The following program example might be used by a bank to update 100 checking accounts. The data for each account consist of the individual's name, account number, old balance, service

charge, and new balance (which becomes the old balance for pur-

poses of the next update). The name is a character string, the

account number is an integer, and the balances are maintained

in floating-point form.

```
CHK_ACC: PROCEDURE OPTIONS (MAIN) ;

        /* EXAMPLE NO. 20 -
           UPDATE 100 CHECKING ACCOUNTS. */

        DECLARE   1 ACCOUNT(100),
                  2 NAME,
                  (3 LAST,
                   3 FIRST)  CHARACTER(12),
                   3 MIDDLE  CHARACTER(2),
                  2 NUMBER   FIXED,
                  (2 OLD_BAL,
                   2 SER_CHG,
                   2 NEW_BAL) FLOAT ;

        /* 'ACCOUNT' CONTAINS DATA FOR EACH OF
           THE 100 ACCOUNTS TO BE UPDATED. */

        DECLARE   1 TOTAL,
                  (2 OLD_BAL,
                   2 NEW_BAL) FLOAT ;

        /* 'TOTAL' WILL CONTAIN THE TOTAL OF THE
           OLD AND NEW BALANCES. */

        DECLARE   1 ED_TOT,
                  (2 OLD_BAL,
                   2 NEW_BAL) PICTURE '$999999V.99' ;

        /* 'ED_TOT' IS USED TO EDIT THE OUTPUT
           FOR PRINTING. */

        DECLARE   I FIXED,
                    DIFF FLOAT ;

        /* READ DATA FOR 100 ACCOUNTS. */

        GET LIST( ACCOUNT ) ;

        /* INITIALIZE OLD AND NEW TOTALS. */

        TOTAL = 0 ;

        /* SUBTRACT SERVICE CHARGE FROM EACH OLD
           BALANCE, GIVING NEW BALANCE. */
```

```
                    ACCOUNT.NEW_BAL = ACCOUNT.OLD_BAL - SER_CHG ;

                    /* SUM THE OLD AND NEW BALANCES IN EACH
                       ACCOUNT. */

LOOP:               DO I = 1 BY 1 TO 100 ;
                       TOTAL.OLD_BAL = TOTAL.OLD_BAL +
                                       ACCOUNT(I).OLD_BAL ;
                       TOTAL.NEW_BAL = TOTAL.NEW_BAL +
                                       ACCOUNT(I).NEW_BAL ;
                    END LOOP ;

                    /* COMPUTE NET GAIN (OR LOSS). */

                    DIFF = TOTAL.NEW_BAL - TOTAL.OLD_BAL ;

                    /* CONVERT TOTALS TO FORM FOR PRINTING. */

                    ED_TOT = TOTAL ;

                    /* PRINT TOTAL OLD BALANCE, TOTAL NEW BALANCE,
                       AND THE DIFFERENCE. */

                    PUT LIST( ED_TOT, DIFF ) ;
                 END CHK_ACC ;
```

The GET statement reads seven elements for each of the
100 accounts into the structure ACCOUNT.

The assignment statement, TOTAL = 0, sets both elements
of the structure TOTAL to zero, element by element. That
statement is equivalent to the statements

```
        TOTAL.OLD_BAL = 0 ; TOTAL.NEW_BAL = 0 ;
```

The DO statement totals the old and new balances in the
structure ACCOUNT, keeping the accumulating totals in the

appropriate elements of the structure TOTAL.

The net gain or loss is then computed as the difference between the total new balance and the total old balance. The difference is computed after the totals have been obtained, although it could have been computed as the sum of the differences of the old and new balance in each of the 100 accounts. By totaling the 100 old and new balances and then taking the difference, the program eliminates 99 computations of the difference.

The data in the structure TOTAL is then placed into the structure EDIT_TOTAL. The PICTURE specification included in the declaration for EDIT_TOTAL specifies that the data are to be converted into a form suitable for printing at the time it is placed in EDIT_TOTAL. The $ in the specification will cause the value printed to be preceded by a dollar sign. By making the assignment to EDIT_TOTAL after the totals have been accumulated, instead of accumulating the totals directly in EDIT_TOTAL, we eliminate 99 conversions.*

---

* In fact, we eliminate many more than 99 conversions. Each time another total is added to EDIT_TOTAL, the existing contents of EDIT_TOTAL must be converted to the form required for the addition, and the sum must then be converted back to the form required by the PICTURE attribute appended to EDIT_TOTAL. Furthermore, every conversion must be performed on each of the two elements of EDIT_TOTAL, further increasing the number of conversions that would be necessary.

Finally, the new information is printed and the update

program terminates.

Example No. 20 contains some statements which are per-

haps unnecessarily complicated, e.g.,


```
TOTAL.OLD_BAL = TOTAL.OLD_BAL + ACCOUNT(I).OLD_BAL ;
```


Wouldn't the program have been much simpler if OLD_BAL

(and NEW_BAL) did not appear in two structures, i.e., if the

names had been made unique so that qualification was not required?

The answer is yes, but to have made the identifiers different might

have introduced some possibility for confusion when reading the

program. However, as we shall now see, there is sometimes

another advantage to using the same identifiers in different

structures.

PL/I provides facilities for structure operations <u>by name</u>.

The general form of specifying operations by name is

<u>statement</u>, BY NAME ;

where <u>statement</u> is an assignment statement which contains only

structures as operands. The clause BY NAME specifies that

only those names which are common to all structures in the statement are to take part in the specified operations.

If the BY NAME clause had been used in Example No. 20 the two statements in the DO loop could be replaced by the statement

```
TOTAL = TOTAL + ACCOUNT(I), BY NAME ;
```

The only items taking part in the addition and assignment would be those having the names OLD_BAL and NEW_BAL, because these are the only names common to the structures TOTAL and ACCOUNT. (Note that there are 100 items with each name in ACCOUNT.)

The decision to use arrays, structures, or a combination of the two depends upon many things. Sometimes, the particular application of a program will dictate a particular organization; at other times, the way the data are to be referenced will be the deciding factor. In general, you should use whatever means makes a program easiest to write.

A structure may be thought of as a list (array), containing sublists which are also arrays. Consider the structure

```
DECLARE   1 CARS,
          2 DOMESTIC,
          3 GM(3),
          3 FORD(3),
          2 FOREIGN(3) ;
```

which could be visualized as

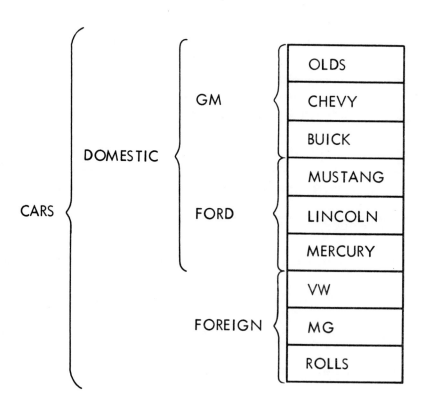

where

> CARS is a 9-element list;

> DOMESTIC is a 6-element list; and

> GM, FORD, and FOREIGN are 3-element lists.

CARS can thus be thought of as a 9-element array containing four other arrays which are proper subsets.* We can refer to any of these subsets, as well as to the entire set (CARS). Suppose we required a list of domestic automobiles as a separate list. We could get it in the following way:

```
DECLARE   DOM(6) CHARACTER(7) ;
  .
  .
DOM = DOMESTIC ;
  .
  .
```

and the array DOM could then be visualized as shown on the following page, i.e., as a contiguous list of six automobiles. There is no distinction within DOM between those automobiles made by GM and those made by FORD. In other words, DOM contains that class of automobiles which are manufactured

---

* It is important to remember that CARS is not in fact an array; it is a structure. Thus, it cannot be subscripted as it could if it were an array.

domestically; a proper subset of the class of all automobiles.

DOM(1)	OLDS
(2)	CHEVY
(3)	BUICK
(4)	MUSTANG
(5)	LINCOLN
(6)	MERCURY

The concept of a structure as containing classes and sub-classes of information is very useful in the discipline of _infor-mation retrieval_. The basic purpose of information retrieval is to collect and classify information so that it can be retrieved on request. The organization of CARS, used as an example here, makes it easy to respond to requests like, "give me a list of domestic automobiles" or "give me a list of automobiles made by General Motors."

One of the major applications of information retrieval is in the maintenance of libraries. The books in a library may be classified by subject, author, content, date of publication, etc. Structures can be of great help in classifying such information.

EXERCISES

5.1   The accounting system for a computer installation is to be

organized as a structure with the name JOB_ACCOUNT,

containing minor elements ACCOUNT_NUMBER, FUNDS,

TIME, and RATE (dollars per unit time used on the com-

puter).   TIME is to be divided into two categories:

COMPILE, and EXECUTE.

a.   Write a DECLARE statement for the structure

JOB_ACCOUNT.

b.   Write a PL/I program, using JOB_ACCOUNT,

which will update the amount of funds left in an

account by means of the formula

$$NEW\_FUNDS \;=\; FUNDS - (RATE * EXECUTE + 0.5*RATE*COMPILE)$$

5.2   Which elements of the structure A will be modified by the

program on the following page?

```
EX2:   PROCEDURE OPTIONS (MAIN) ;

            DECLARE   1 A,
                        2 R,
                        2 S,
                          3 T,
                          3 U,
                        2 V,
                          3 W ;

            DECLARE   1 B,
                        2 S,
                          3 T,
                        2 W ;

        A = B, BY NAME ;

     END EX2 ;
```

5.3   A library contains 770 books which are broadly

classified as fiction and non-fiction. The fiction class

is divided into two classes: novels (275 books) and short

stories (200). The non-fiction class is divided into three

classes: biography (125), documentary (70), and general

reference (100).

a.   Declare a structure, BOOKS, which contains

the appropriate classifications.

b.   Write a PL/I program, using the structure

which reads a character string which will be

one of the following

'FICTION'   'BIOGRAPHY'

'NONFICTION'   'DOCUMENTARY'

'NOVELS'   'REFERENCE'

'SHORT STORIES'

and prints a list of those books which fit the

indicated classification.   Assume that the

longest book title is 10 characters.

CHAPTER 6

INPUT/OUTPUT

There are three basic phases in every computer program:

1. Acquire data

2. Process data

3. Communicate results

Up to this point we have concentrated on phase 2, the processing phase, and have shown some of the facilities in PL/I that can be used during this phase. We have not paid much attention to phases 1 and 3, although they are essential if a program is to be at all useful.

There are two ways in which a program can acquire the data that are to be processed. One way is for the program to generate its own data during execution, and the other is for it to read the data by means of GET statements. Most programs use a combination of these two methods.

There are many ways in which a program can communicate

results. For example, results can be printed in order to com-

municate with a human being; they can be punched into cards

which can subsequently be read by another program; etc. The

basic statement used to communicate results is the PUT state-

ment, which has been used in the programming examples.

GET and PUT statements perform "input" and "output"

functions, respectively. In practice, input and output are fre-

quently considered to be a single function, input/output, (or,

simply, I/O) because there are many similarities in the way

the functions are implemented in most programming languages.

For example, the statement

```
GET LIST( A, B, C ) ;
```

causes three data items to be read into the computer from, say,

a punched card, and assigned to A, B, and C. The very similar

statement

```
PUT LIST( A, B, C ) ;
```

causes the values of A, B, and C to be written out from the

computer to, say, the printer.

In short, GET statements cause data to be transmitted to

the computer from an external device, and PUT statements cause data to be transmitted from the computer to an external device. Some external devices can be used both for input and output; some can be used only for input; and some can be used only for output. The table below lists some typical external devices and shows how they can be used.

Device	Use
Card reader	Input
Card punch	Output
Printer	Output
Magnetic tape	Input/Output
Typewriter	Input/Output
Graphic display	Input/Output

Collections of data on external devices are called <u>files</u>. GET statements extract data from an input file, and PUT statements place data into an output file. PL/I programs can use several input files and several output files. We will assume for the moment that they use only one of each, called the "standard" files. We will also assume that the output file is a printer.

Three kinds of GET and PUT statements are used in PL/I. Each kind of statement specifies a particular representation of the data in a file. The three kinds of statements and their general forms are

List-directed

GET LIST(list) ;

PUT LIST(list) ;

Data-directed

GET DATA(list) ;   or   GET DATA ;

PUT DATA(list) ;

Edit-directed

GET EDIT(list) (format) ;

PUT EDIT(list) (format) ;

In every case above, list is a sequence of items separated by commas. The form of each item depends on the kind of statement in use; permissible forms are summarized in the table on page 181. In the case of edit-directed input/output, format specifies the form of the data in a file. Formats are discussed in detail later in this chapter.

For input, the kind of GET statement used depends on how the data are represented in the input file. For output, the kind of PUT statement used depends on how it is desired to represent the data in the output file. In both cases, data representation involves 1) the form of each data item, and 2) the way in which data items are separated from one another, or "delimited." The representations specified by the three kinds of GET and PUT statements are:

DATA REPRESENTATION IN A FILE

	form of each item	items delimited by . . .
List-directed	constant	one or more blanks, or a comma
Data-directed	variable = constant	one or more blanks, or a comma*
Edit-directed	characters, inter-preted by format specifications	format speci-fications

* A semicolon must follow the last item when the data are in the input file.

Suppose a PL/I program contains the statements

```
DECLARE  VAR1     FIXED(2,1),
         VAR2     FIXED(2),
         ANIMAL   CHARACTER(3) ;

L: GET LIST( VAR1, VAR2, ANIMAL ) ;
```

and the input file contains

1.5,   -83,   'CAT',   -3.0, -85,   'DOG'

The first time the GET statement is executed, VAR1 will be set to 1.5, VAR2 will be set to -83, and ANIMAL will be set to the character string CAT. If the GET statement is executed a second time, VAR1 will be set to 3.0, VAR2 will be set to -85, and ANIMAL will be set to the character string DOG. Every time the GET statement is executed, three data items are taken from the input file and assigned to the variables in the associated list.

Usually, if the list in a GET statement contains n identifiers, n data items will be extracted from the input file each time the statement is executed. However, a single identifier may cause input of more than one item. For example,

```
DECLARE  A(10) FIXED ;
  •
  •
  •
GET LIST( A ) ;
```

will extract ten items from the input file and assign them to the

elements of the array A. The first item will be assigned to

A(1) and the tenth will be assigned to A(10).

Once started, list-directed input can be terminated in two

ways: satisfaction of the input list, or by an "end of file"

condition. The latter is "raised" when there are no more data

in the file, and usually causes program execution to terminate.*

Unless the condition is raised, the computer will scan the input

file as far as necessary to satisfy the input list. There must be

one blank space or a comma between data items in the file, but

intervening blanks are otherwise ignored.

There are several differences between list-directed input

and list-directed output. For input, the list (list in the state-

ment on page 159) may contain identifiers only, although the

_____

* Chapter 9 describes a means by which programs can detect
the ENDFILE condition and take various courses of action when
it is raised.

identifiers may be subscripted if appropriate. For output, the list may contain constants and expressions as well. Constants in an output list are placed in the output file in the same form as they appear in the list, but without the quote marks in the case of string constants. In the case of expressions, the values placed in the output file are those resulting from their evaluation.

During input, data items from the input file are converted to the form required by the attributes of the corresponding variables in the input list. If such an item is subsequently placed in the output file, it will be placed there in its converted form. For example,

Input -1.5

```
DECLARE X FIXED(5,3) ;
GET LIST( X ) ;
PUT LIST( X ) ;
```

Output -1.500

List-directed output can be terminated only by exhaustion of the output list. (Note that an input list is said to be "satisfied" but an output list is said to be "exhausted.") The ENDFILE condition cannot be raised during output.

List-directed input/output derives its name from the fact that data to be transmitted are specified in an input or output list in terms of their destination (input) or in terms of their source (output). The input and output files contain only the values of the items.

The second kind of input/output described in this chapter, data-directed input/output, differs from list-directed input/output in that the input and output files contain not only the values of data items, but also the PL/I program names with which the values are associated. Suppose, for example, a PL/I program contains the statements

```
DECLARE   A FIXED,
          B FLOAT,
          C CHARACTER(3) ;

    L: GET DATA ;
```

and the input file contains

```
C = 'CAT', A = 4, B = 6.5 ; C = 'DOG' ;
```

The first time the GET statement is executed, the variable A will be set to 4, B will be set to 6.5, and C will be set to the character string CAT. Transmission is terminated by the semicolon in the input file. If the GET statement is executed a second time, the effect will be to change the value of the variable C to the character string DOG. The following semicolon terminates transmission and, since A and B do not appear prior to the semicolon, their values are not altered by the GET statement the second time.

When the list is omitted from a data-directed GET statement, as it is in the illustration on the preceding page, the input file can contain assignments to any of the variables in the program. As shown on page 159 however, a list (exactly like the list used with a list-directed GET statement) may be used with a data-directed GET statement. When a list is used, the input file may specify assignments to any or all of the identifiers in the list, but not necessarily in the same order. The input file must not, however, specify assignment to any identifiers that are not in the list. Thus, a data-directed input list normally specifies those variables whose values could be changed by the particular GET statement.

The variable in an "assignment statement" in the input file must be a simple variable; an array name with all subscripts specified by decimal integer constants, i.e., a single element of an array; or a _fully_ qualified elementary name, i.e., a single element of a structure. The list, if used, may contain simple variables, unsubscripted array names, and major or partially qualified structure names. In the latter cases, the input file may specify assignment to any or all of the elements of the array or structure.

In data-directed output, the names of the sources of the data items are placed into the output file together with the items themselves. A list, specifying the sources, must be used with data-directed PUT statements exactly as with list-directed PUT statements. However, a data-directed output list may contain identifiers only; it may not contain constants or expressions. A semicolon is placed in the output file after the last data item has been transmitted.

The third kind of input/output described in this chapter, _edit_-directed input/output, differs from list- and data-directed input/output in that it specifies the format of the input and output files and provides means for editing the transmitted data.

In order to understand edit-directed input/output, it is useful to think of the input and output files as being streams of characters, where every character in the stream - including

blanks - is accounted for by a "format specification." During

input, characters are accessed from the input stream and inter-

preted according to the format specifications; during output,

characters are placed into the output stream according to the

specifications.

The edit-directed input/output statements have the form

GET EDIT(list) (format) ;

PUT EDIT(list) (format) ;

where list is like the list used with list-directed GET and PUT

statements, respectively; and format is a series of editing speci-

fications, called "format phrases," which specify the form of

the data in the input file, or the desired form of the data in the

output file, i.e., on a printed page.

Suppose a PL/I program contains the statement

```
DECLARE P CHARACTER(5),
        Q FIXED(5) ;
```

and that it is desired to access a ten-character substream of the

input data stream in the following way: place the first five char-

acters into P as a character string, ignore the next two characters, and interpret the next three characters as a decimal integer and assign it to Q. The PL/I statement would be

GET EDIT(P, Q) (A(5), X(2), F(3)) ;

The "A" format phrase specifies that the input data are to be interpreted as a character string. The "5" specifies the number of characters that are to be so interpreted. Thus, the phrase A(5) specifies that the first data item is to be interpreted as a five-character string. The string is assigned to the variable P because P is the first identifier in the input list and A(5) is the first editing phrase.

The "X" phrase specifies that a certain number of characters - two, in this case - are to be ignored. The X phrase does not cause any transmission; it merely advances the input stream by the specified number of characters.

The "F" phrase specifies that the input data are to be interpreted as a fixed-point number. The "3" specifies the number of characters that are to be interpreted to form the number. It does not specify the precision of the number. The number is then assigned to the variable Q because Q is the next identifier in the list. Note: If the three-character number is negative, it can have at most two digits because the minus sign occupies a character position in the input stream. Numbers in the range -99 to 999 can be transmitted by the format phrase F(3).

Some of the more frequently used format phrases are listed below, with their meanings. Additional phrases are given in Appendix F. Note that some of the phrases may have a different form and/or meaning when used for input than they do when used for output.

Phrase		Meaning
A(w)	INPUT:	Interpret the next w characters as a character string.
	OUTPUT:	Place the associated item into the output stream as a character string of length w. If w is omitted, it is assumed to be the current length of the item. If w is greater than the length of the item, the item will be left-justified in a w-character substream, followed by blanks.
E(w, d)	INPUT:	Interpret the next w characters as a floating-point number written in scientific notation (see Chapter 1).

169

E(w, d)   If none of the characters is
                           a decimal point, assume the
                           decimal point precedes the
                           rightmost d digits in the field.

               OUTPUT: Place the associated item into
                           the output stream as a float-
                           ing-point number written in
                           scientific notation. If the
                           item requires less than w
                           characters, it will be right-
                           justified in a w-character
                           substream, preceded by
                           blanks. The general form of
                           output data edited by the E
                           phrase is

                                n. nnnEnn

                           (one digit to the left of the
                           decimal point, and d digits
                           to the right). Either or
                           both the exponent and the
                           magnitude will be preceded
                           by a minus sign, if appro-
                           priate.

F(w)   INPUT: Interpret the next w charac-
                           ters as a fixed-point number.
  or   If none of the characters is a
                           decimal point, assume the
F(w, d)   decimal point precedes the
                           rightmost d digits. If d is
                           omitted, it is taken to be 0.

               OUTPUT: Place the associated item into
                           the output stream as a fixed-
                           point number with d digits to
                           the right of the decimal point.
                           If the item requires less than
                           w characters, it will be right-

170

F(w) or F(w, d)	justified in a w-character substream, preceded by blanks. Leading zeroes, if any, will be suppressed, i.e., converted to blanks. If d is omitted, no decimal point will appear in the number. If d is 0, no digits will follow the decimal point, but the point will be printed.

X(w)   INPUT: Ignore the next w characters in the input stream.

OUTPUT: Insert w blanks into the output stream.

During output, it is not always necessary to use the X phrase to insert blanks into the output stream, because data edited by the E and F phrases may be preceded by blanks. For example, the phrase F(15) is equivalent to (X(5), F(10)), assuming the associated data item as printed will not have more than ten digits.

The field width, w, specified for the E and F phrases must account for all of the characters to be printed. The E phrase requires that w be at least d+7 to account for

a leading sign (1 character)

at least one digit

the decimal point (1 character)

171

the letter "E" (1 character)

the sign of the exponent (1 character)

the exponent (2 characters)

The F phrase must allow for the decimal point, if it is to

appear, and a leading sign.

Suppose a PL/I program contains the following statement:

```
DECLARE   A   CHARACTER(3)    INITIAL( 'CAT' ),
          B   FLOAT           INITIAL( 1.25 ),
          C   FLOAT           INITIAL( -6.5 ) ;
```

and the statement

PUT EDIT(A, B, C) (...) ;

is executed with (...) replaced by each of the formats shown

on the following page. The printed results actually produced by

a computer are shown to the right of each format specification.

The form of data in a file can also be specified in a way

similar to a PICTURE specification, by means of the P format

phrase. The general form of the P phrase is

P'specifications'

where specifications consist of a sequence of characters repre-

FORMAT	PRINTED RESULTS
(A, F(4,2), F(4,1)) ;	CAT1.25-6.5
(A(10), F(4,2), F(6,1)) ;	CAT 1.25 -6.5
(A, X(5), F(4,2), E(7,1)) ;	CAT 1.25-.6E+01
(A, F(10,1), E(10,1)) ;	CAT 1.2 -.6E+01
(A, E(10,1), E(15,6)) ;	CAT .1E+01 -.650000E+01

senting a symbolic "picture" of the data in a file. Some of the more frequently used specification characters are listed below. Additional specification characters are given in Appendix F.

Specification character	Meaning
9	The corresponding character may be any decimal digit, or blank.
A	The corresponding character may be any alphabetic character, or blank.
X	The corresponding character may be any character.
V	A decimal point should be assumed at the corresponding point in the item. V does not specify the appearance of an actual decimal point in an item.

The above characters may be used both for input and output. The following characters may be used for output:

Specification character	Meaning
B	A blank is to be inserted in the output stream.
S	A sign (+ or -) is to be inserted at the corresponding point in the item.

Z	If the associated character is a leading zero (a zero to the left of a non-zero digit) it will be replaced by a blank.
*	Same as Z, above, except that a leading zero will be replaced by an asterisk.
+	If the associated item is greater than or equal to zero, a plus sign is to be inserted at the corresponding point in the output stream. Otherwise, no sign will appear.
-	Same as +, above, except that a sign will appear only if the associated item is less than zero.
.	A decimal point is to be inserted at the corresponding point in the item.
$	A dollar sign is to be inserted at the corresponding point in the item.

The characters S, +, -, and $ can be made to "drift" so that they will appear immediately to the left of the first non-blank character in the output stream. This is important, for instance, when printing checks, to prevent them from being "kited" (raised in value) by the insertion of spurious high order digits between the $ and the original amount of the check. A drifting character is specified by the appearance of the appropriate character in each position through which it may drift. For example, the specification

$$P'\$\$\$\$\$9.99'$$

could be used to print a value from \$0.00 to \$9999.99 with no spaces between the \$ and the first significant digit.

Suppose a PL/I program contains the following statement:

```
DECLARE   A   CHARACTER(3)    INITIAL( 'CAT' ),
          B   FLOAT           INITIAL( 1.25 ),
          C   FLOAT           INITIAL( -6.5 ) ;
```

and the statement

$$\text{PUT EDIT(A, B, C) (...) ;}$$

is executed with (...) replaced by each of the formats shown on the following page. The printed results actually produced by a computer are shown to the right of each format specification. Note that the P phrase can used in combination with the other format phrases described previously.

A format phrase may be preceded by a replication factor which specifies that the phrase is to be repeated a certain number of times. For example, the phrase

$$(5)F(6,2)$$

FORMAT	PRINTED RESULTS
(A, P'9V.99', P'S9V.9') ;	CAT1.25-6.5
(A, P'999V.9', P'ZZZV.99') ;	CAT001.2 6.50
(P'AAA', X(3), P'$$$9V.99', P'SSS9V.9') ;	CAT $1.25 -6.5
(A, P'--9V.99', P'+++9V.99') ;	CAT 1.25 6.50
(P'(10)A', 2P'XXXXXX') ;	CAT 1.250-6.500

specifies that five consecutive data items are to be edited by the phrase F(6, 2).

With the exception of the P phrase, format phrases have the general form

$$(\underline{r}) \ \underline{phrase} \ (\underline{w}, \underline{d})$$

where

    $\underline{r}$ is a replication factor;

    $\underline{phrase}$ is one of the letters A, E, F, or X;

    $\underline{w}$ is the total number of characters in the associated item;

    $\underline{d}$, if used, specifies the number of digits to the right of the decimal point in an arithmetic item.

Any of the components, $\underline{r}$, $\underline{w}$, and $\underline{d}$, may be decimal integer constants, or they may be expressions.* The use of expressions can frequently simplify PL/I programs considerably. For example, suppose it is desired to read a character string of length "N" where N is in the input stream as a three-character number preceding the string. The GET statement might be

```
GET EDIT( N, STRING ) ( F(3), A(N) ) ;
```

---

* If $\underline{r}$ is a decimal integer constant it need not be parenthesized.

A format need not contain as many editing phrases as there are items in the associated list. If the format contains fewer editing phrases than there are items in the list, the format is repeated as necessary to transmit all the data. As in list- and data-directed input/output, transmission stops only when the list is satisfied or exhausted. The statement

PUT EDIT(P, Q, R) (F(5,2), X(5), E(10,2), X(3)) ;

will cause the value of P to be edited by the phrase F(5, 2), the value of Q to be edited by the phrase E(10, 2), and the value of R to be edited by the phrase F(5, 2). There will be five blanks between the values of P and Q, and three blanks between the values of Q and R as they are printed.

Format specifications can be very complicated when many data items are to be transmitted. Also, it is not always easy to write a list of items and then write the format specifications for the entire list. In edit-directed input/output, lists and format specifications can be intermixed; the general form of such a GET or PUT statement is

EDIT(list) (format) (list) (format) ... ;

179

where each _format_ is associated with the _list_ to its left. Each

list-format pair interacts to transmit a certain amount of data.

As each list is exhausted, transmission continues using the next

list-format pair to the right. Program example 25 on page 192

illustrates a simple way of putting a large amount of data into a

rather complicated printed format.

Edit-directed input/output, together with list- and data-

directed input/output, constitute the "stream input/output"

facilities of PL/I because the files can be thought of as streams

from which data are extracted during input, or into which data

are inserted during output. Much of the remainder of this chap-

ter applies to all three forms of stream input/output, so it is

useful to review briefly their various characteristics. Each of

the three forms specifies a particular representation of data in

a file, as shown in the table on page 160. With the possible

exception of a data-directed input statement, every input/output

statement has a list of data items associated with it. The per-

missible contents of input/output lists are summarized in the

table on the following page.

Unless otherwise stated, the following discussion applies

to all three forms of stream input/output statements. Where a particular form, e.g., LIST, is used, the choice is arbitrary; DATA or EDIT could be used just as well.

CONTENTS OF I/O LISTS

	Input	Output
List-directed	identifiers	identifiers, constants, and expressions
Data-directed	identifiers	identifiers
Edit-directed	identifiers	identifiers, constants, and expressions

Data items taken from the input file cannot be assigned to PL/I program variables directly. First, they must be converted to the computer's internal form. Then, possibly, they must be further converted so that they match the attributes declared for the variables that are to receive them. Suppose a PL/I program contains the statements

```
DECLARE ( A, B, C ) FIXED(5,3) ;
GET LIST( A, B, C ) ;
```

and that the input file contains

$$1.5, \ -1.0625, \ 'XYZ'$$

The first data item in the file consists of three characters: the digit "1", a period, and the digit "5". These characters are converted to the internal equivalent of the fixed-point decimal quantity 1.5; a quantity having precision (2, 1). The quantity is then further converted to precision (5, 3) - the precision attribute of A, the destination - by the addition of leading and trailing zeroes.*

The second data item in the file is converted in the same way, to the internal equivalent of the quantity -1.0625, with precision (5, 4). It is then further converted to precision (5, 3) - the precision attribute of B - by truncating the extra digit to the right of the decimal point, and adding a leading zero. The value assigned to B is thus effectively -1.062 .

The third data item in the file is first converted to the internal form of the character string XYZ. This string must then be converted to a fixed-decimal number of precision (5, 3),

---

* If the value of A is subsequently printed by a list-directed PUT statement, leading zeroes will be suppressed. See page 163.

but there is no way in which a character string can be converted to a meaningful numeric quantity (unless the characters happen to be digits). The attempted conversion will raise the "conversion" condition, which will normally terminate program execution. Chapter 9 describes a means by which programs can detect the CONVERSION condition and take various courses of action when it is raised.

When using edit-directed input, the internal equivalent of a data item is formed from the format specifications instead of from the appearance of the item in the file. The equivalent may then be further converted before assignment, as described above.

During output, data items are converted to external form as defined by their attributes. That is, an item declared to have precision (5,3) will be placed in the output file as a five-digit number with three digits following the decimal point. When using edit-directed output, data items are converted to the form specified by the associated format phrases. The end result is that characters are placed in the output file to be printed. Any kind of data can be converted to a character string, so the CONVERSION condition cannot be raised during output.

It is frequently very useful to print the data read by GET statements, particularly when many data items are involved. Up to this point, we have printed the input data by means of PUT statements, along with the results of the calculation. The COPY option can be used with a GET statement to provide for automatic printout of the input data. The general form of a GET statement with the COPY option is

GET COPY LIST(list) ;

or

GET LIST(list) COPY ;

where LIST is used only for illustration; COPY can be used with data- and edit-directed input as well.

The COPY option does not indicate which values were assigned to which variables, or what conversions, if any, were performed prior to assignment. Thus, it may sometimes be preferable to check the input data by means of a PUT statement immediately following the GET statement.

Three options may be used with PUT statements to provide control over the printer. The general form of a PUT statement with an option is similar to the form of a GET statement with an option; the option may appear after PUT, or before the semicolon. The three PUT options are

Option	Effect
SKIP or SKIP(w)	Space the printer to a new print line, and print the data starting at the left margin. If w is 0 or negative, printing will start at the left of the current line, over-printing any data previously printed on the line. If w is 1, or is omitted, the printer is spaced to the next line, giving single-spaced printing. If w is 2, printing will be double-spaced, etc.
LINE(w)	Space the printer to line w on the print page, and print the data starting at the left margin. LINE specifies a skip to a specified line on the page, while SKIP, above, specifies a skip to a new line relative to the current line.
PAGE	Eject the current page. The data will be printed starting at the left margin of the first line (line 1) of the next page.
Note:	LINE(w) is equivalent to PAGE if w is less than the number of the current line, is less than 1, or is greater than the maximum number of lines that can appear on a page.

PUT options always specify an action to be taken by the printer before any data are transmitted. A PUT statement with an option need not cause any transmission at all; the statement

```
PUT PAGE ;
```

merely causes the printer to skip to the top of the next page.

The following two program examples perform the same functions: summing five numbers and printing them, together with the total. The major difference between the programs is that Example No. 22 uses PUT options, while Example No. 21 does not. The input data are the same in both cases, and both programs use the SUM function, which is a built-in function described in Appendix C.

```
SUM1: PROCEDURE OPTIONS (MAIN) ;

        /* EXAMPLE NO. 21
           SUM FIVE NUMBERS. PRINT RESULTS WITHOUT
           'PUT' OPTIONS. */

        DECLARE (A(5), TOTAL) FIXED DECIMAL(5,2) ;

        GET LIST( A ) ;
        TOTAL = SUM( A ) ;
        PUT LIST( 'OUTPUT FROM EXAMPLE NO. 21' ) ;
        PUT LIST( A, 'TOTAL = ', TOTAL ) ;
    END SUM1 ;
```

```
OUTPUT FROM EXAMPLE NO. 21


   10.20     5.30     75.00     1.05     2.00 TOTAL =     93.54
```

```
SUM2: PROCEDURE OPTIONS (MAIN) ;

        /* EXAMPLE NO. 22
           SUM FIVE NUMBERS. PRINT RESULTS USING
           'PUT' OPTIONS. */

        DECLARE (A(5), TOTAL) FIXED DECIMAL(5,2) ,
                I FIXED ;

        GET LIST( A ) ;
        TOTAL = SUM( A ) ;

        PUT LIST( 'OUTPUT FROM EXAMPLE NO. 22' ) PAGE ;
        PUT SKIP(2) ;

        DO I = 1 TO 5 ;
           PUT LIST( A(I) ) SKIP ;
        END ;

        PUT LIST ( '      _____' ) SKIP(0) ; /* FIVE UNDERBARS */
        PUT LIST( TOTAL ) SKIP ;
     END SUM2 ;
```

                    OUTPUT FROM EXAMPLE NO. 22

                         10.20
                          5.30
                         75.00
                          1.05
                          2.00
                         93.54

SKIP, LINE, and PAGE may also be used as format phrases

in edit-directed PUT statements. In this context, they have the

same effects as they do when used as options, except that the

specified action occurs when they are encountered in the format.

Another format phrase that can be used with edit-directed PUT statements is the COLUMN phrase, which has the form

COLUMN(w)

and causes the next data item to be printed beginning at position w of the current print line. If w exceeds the number of positions available on a line, or is less than the current position on the current print line, COLUMN is equivalent to SKIP(1). COLUMN may not be used as an option.

As we have seen, input and output of an entire array can be accomplished simply by placing the array name in an input or output list. In many cases, it is useful to transmit only part of an array, e.g., the first "N" elements. A typical application might be to sum a list of numbers where there are N numbers in the list. Example No. 23 on the following page shows how this might be done for an arbitrary number of lists, when each list is preceded by an integer specifying its length. The numbers in each list are placed into the first "N" elements of an array by means of a repetitive specification, which is described following the example.

```
SUM3:  PROCEDURE OPTIONS (MAIN) ;

          /* EXAMPLE NO. 23
             SUM LISTS OF NUMBERS. EACH LIST IS PRECEDED
             BY THE NUMBER OF ITEMS IN THE LIST.  TERMINATE
             WHEN THAT NUMBER IS ZERO. */

          DECLARE ( I, N, NUMBER(1000), TOTAL ) FIXED ;

START:    GET LIST( N, (NUMBER(I) DO I = 1 TO N) ) ;
          IF N=0 THEN GO TO STOP ;

          TOTAL = NUMBER(1) ; /* INITIALIZE FOR SUM. */
LOOP:     DO I = 2 TO N ;
             TOTAL = TOTAL + NUMBER(I) ;
          END LOOP ;

          PUT LIST( (NUMBER(I) DO I = 1 TO N), TOTAL ) ;
          GO TO START ;

STOP:     PUT LIST( 'END OF JOB' ) ;
          END SUM3 ;
```

The repetitive specification in the GET and PUT statements in Example No. 23 is the construction

$$(\text{NUMBER(I)} \ \text{DO} \ I = 1 \ \text{TO} \ 10)$$

which specifies that the Ith element of the array NUMBER is to be transmitted for each value of I from 1 to N (in steps of 1).

Repetitive specifications are similar to DO loops in many ways; a repetitive specification is essentially a DO loop applied to items in an input or output list. Like DO loops, which can control any number of statements, repetitive specifications can be applied to any number of items in an input or output list. For example, the statement

```
PUT LIST( (A(I), B(I) DO I = 1 BY 2 TO 9) ) ;
```

will cause data to be transmitted from arrays A and B in the sequence A(1), B(1), A(3), B(3), ... A(9), B(9). In general, repetitive specifications have the form

(<u>list</u> DO <u>specifications</u>)

where <u>list</u> is a list of items that are permissible in the list in which the repetitive specification appears, and <u>specifications</u> are as defined in Chapter 4.

Items in <u>list</u> can themselves be repetitive specifications; the effect is the same as nesting DO loops. The statement

```
GET LIST( ((A(I,J) DO J = 1 TO 10) DO I = 1 TO 10) ) ;
```

is equivalent to

```
DO I = 1 TO 10 ;
    DO J = 1 TO 10 ;
        GET LIST( A(I,J) ) ;
    END ;
END ;
```

which is equivalent to

```
GET LIST( A ) ;
```

provided that A is declared with the dimension attribute (10, 10).

Finally, like DO loops, repetitive specifications are frequently, but not necessarily, used when working with arrays. The following one-statement program performs the same function as Example No. 15 (page 116), namely, to print a table of sines:

```
SINE: PROCEDURE OPTIONS (MAIN) ;
        /* EXAMPLE NO. 24
           PRINT TABLE OF SINES, PERFORMING ALL COMPU-
           TATIONS IN A 'PUT' STATEMENT. */
        DECLARE X FLOAT ;
        PUT LIST( (X, SIN(X)   DO X = 0 BY 0.1 TO 6.28) ) ;
        END SINE ;
```

The following example program reads data representing a company's monthly sales figures for the years 1963, 1964, and 1965, totals the sales for each year, and prints the results in tabular form. The program uses list-directed input because the data need not appear in any particular format (this convenience would not likely exist in a real-life situation) and list-directed data is the simplest to prepare. The program uses edit-directed

191

input to read three-character abbreviations for the months of
the year, because the 36 characters were most convenient to
prepare as a 36-character string. All output is edit-directed
in order to prepare a neat table.

```
XYZ_4:     PROCEDURE OPTIONS (MAIN) ;

           /* EXAMPLE NO. 25
              XYZ COMPANY, SALES TOTALS FOR 1963-65. */

           DECLARE   SALES( 12,1963:1965) FIXED(5),
                     TOTALS(1963:1965) FIXED(5),
                     MONTH(12) CHARACTER(3),
                     (I, J) FIXED BINARY ;

           /* START OFF WITH NEW PAGE. */
           PUT PAGE ;

           /* HEAD EACH COLUMN WITH YEAR. */
           PUT EDIT( 1963, 1964, 1965 ) ( F(17), 2F(10) ) ;

           /* INSERT ONE ADDITIONAL SPACE. */
           PUT SKIP ;

           /* BRING IN DATA FOR ARRAY 'MONTH.' */
           GET EDIT( MONTH ) ( 12A(3) ) ;

           /* BRING IN SALES DATA. */
           GET LIST( ((SALES(I,J) DO J = 1963 TO 1965)
                               DO I = 1 TO 12) ) ;

           TOTALS = 0 ;

           /* PRINT TABLE AND COMPUTE TOTALS. */

L1:        DO I = 1 TO 12 ;
               PUT EDIT( MONTH(I) ) ( SKIP, A(7) )
                        ( ( SALES(I,J) DO J = 1963 TO 1965) )
                        ( 3F(10) ) ;
L2:            DO J = 1963, 1964, 1965 ;
                   TOTALS(J) = TOTALS(J) + SALES(I,J) ;
               END L2 ;
           END L1 ;

           /* PRINT TOTALS. */

           PUT EDIT( 'TOTALS', TOTALS )
                   ( SKIP(2), A, F(11), 2F(10) ) ;

       END XYZ_4 ;
```

192

Input data to Example No. 25:

```
JANFEBMARAPRMAYJUNJULAUGSEPOCTNOVDEC
120  234  186  199  204  213  208  197  253  244  245  196
179  208  202  196  244  244  256  199  218  223  230  239
226  246  230  247  253  255  229  246  249  253  258  263
```

Output from Example No. 25:

	1963	1964	1965
JAN	120	234	186
FEB	199	204	213
MAR	208	197	253
APR	244	245	196
MAY	179	208	202
JUN	196	244	244
JUL	256	199	218
AUG	223	230	239
SEP	226	246	230
OCT	247	253	255
NOV	229	246	249
DEC	253	258	263
TOTALS	2580	2764	2748

Conceptually, the input and output files are character
strings (in which redundant blanks are ignored during list-
and data-directed input), and are in many ways similar to PL/I
character string variables. Can data be read from and written
into character string variables instead of the standard files?
Yes, and the facility can be a very useful one.

Data in the input file cannot be read more than once. If it

193

is necessary to read the same data more than once, the items

can be taken from the input file and placed in a character string

variable by means of an appropriate GET statement. Subse-

quently, and as often as necessary, the data can then be read

from the string by means of other GET statements. A typical

problem might be to interpret the next 50 characters in the

input file first as ten 5-digit integers, and again as five 10-digit

integers. Here is a solution:

```
DECLARE  A(10)     FIXED(5),
         B(5)      FIXED(10),
         BUFFER    CHARACTER(50) ;

/* READ 50 CHARACTERS INTO 'BUFFER' */

GET EDIT( BUFFER ) ( A(50) ) ;

/* INTERPRET CHARACTERS AS 10 FIVE-DIGIT
   INTEGERS; STORE IN ARRAY 'A' */

GET STRING( BUFFER ) EDIT( A ) ( 10F(5) ) ;

/* INTERPRET CHARACTERS AS 5 TEN-DIGIT
   INTEGERS; STORE IN ARRAY 'B' */

GET STRING( BUFFER ) EDIT( B ) ( 5F(10) ) ;
```

The first GET statement above is a typical GET statement

which places the next 50 characters from the input file into the

character string variable BUFFER.

The other two GET statements use the STRING option,

which specifies that data are to be taken not from the input file, but from a character string variable in the program. In this case, the variable is BUFFER.

The STRING option may also be used with PUT statements to specify that data are to be transmitted to a character string variable instead of to the output file. The following example program reads five 80-character groups from the input file; each group is preceded by a number from 1 to 5, and then prints the groups in sequence, one group per line. Such a process is not unusual when using a computer to prepare reports.

```
REPORT:  PROCEDURE OPTIONS (MAIN) ;
               /* EXAMPLE NO. 26
                  READ LINES FOR A REPORT, PUT THEM IN
                  SEQUENCE, AND PRINT THE REPORT. */

               DECLARE   ( I, LINE_NO ) FIXED,
                          IMAGE(5)          CHARACTER(80),
                          GROUP             CHARACTER(80) ;

               DO I = 1 TO 5 ;

                    /* BRING IN A GROUP */
                    GET LIST( LINE_NO, GROUP ) ;

                    /* PUT GROUP INTO REPORT IMAGE */
                    PUT STRING( IMAGE(LINE_NO) ) EDIT( GROUP )
                                                     ( A(80) ) ;

               END ;

               /* PRINT THE REPORT */
               PUT EDIT( IMAGE ) ( SKIP, A ) ;

          END REPORT ;
```

The following general rules apply when the STRING option is used:

1. Data are transmitted to or from the string beginning with the first character of the string.

2. Data placed in a string by a list-, data-, or edit-directed PUT statement can be accessed by a list-, data-, or edit-directed GET statement, respectively.

3. When used in a PUT statement, no other options may appear, nor may SKIP, PAGE, LINE, or COLUMN appear as format phrases.

4. The string referenced by a PUT statement must be long enough to hold all of the data. Remember that certain characters, e.g., a decimal point can be inserted during output conversion.

The input/output facilities that have been presented in this chapter are designed primarily for communication between the computer and the people who use it. Although all programs will use some of the facilities described here, PL/I contains many additional input/output facilities that can be used when it is unnecessary to convert data from internal to external form. These facilities are described in Chapter 11.

1. Stream files are read and written by GET and PUT

    statements, respectively. It is a common error to

    attempt to use READ and WRITE for these purposes,

    but these words have totally different functions in PL/I.

    They are described in Chapter 11.

2. It sometimes happens that a certain series of format

    phrases can be used with many GET and/or PUT

    statements in a program. Rather than write each

    such series each time it is to be used, it can be writ-

    ten once and placed in the program remotely from the

    statements that reference it. The general form of a

    remotely specified format is

    label: FORMAT(specifications) ;

    and the specifications can then be referenced by means

    of the "R" format phrase in a format associated with a

    GET or PUT statement. The general form of the R for-

    mat phrase is

    R(label) ;

where label is the label of a FORMAT statement. The program example below illustrates the use of remote format specifications. The problem is to read ten floating-point numbers into each of two arrays, A and B, and print their contents and the sum of corresponding elements.

```
RFORM:      PROCEDURE OPTIONS (MAIN) ;

                /* EXAMPLE NO. 27
                   ILLUSTRATE REMOTE FORMATS. */

                DECLARE (A, B)(10) FIXED(10,3) ;
F1:             FORMAT( 10F(10,3) ) ;
F2:             FORMAT( A, R(F1) ) ;
F3:             FORMAT( SKIP, X(5), R(F2) ) ;

                GET EDIT( A, B ) ( R(F1) ) ;

                PUT EDIT( 'A = ', A ) ( PAGE, R(F3) ) ;
                PUT EDIT( 'B = ', B ) ( R(F3) ) ;
                PUT EDIT( 'TOTAL = ', A+B ) ( SKIP(2), X(1), R(F2) ) ;
            END RFORM ;
```

The example illustrates the fact that remote formats may themselves contain R phrases. However, no format may reference itself with an R phrase, nor may it reference another format that in turn references it. The phrase R(F3), for instance, would be illegal in any of the formats F1, F2, and F3 because it would result in "circular" nesting of formats, regardless of which of the three is referenced by a GET or PUT statement.

The SKIP option may be used with a GET statement. When this is done, a new card is read immediately. Data are then transmitted as usual for stream input. Note that the next card is read before any data are transmitted. In some cases this may require the use of a blank card preceding the data deck.

EXERCISES

6.1   Name four ways in which a value can be assigned to a character string variable.

6.2   Modify Example No. 4 (page 41) to use data-directed output.

6.3   Why would data-directed input/output be awkward in Example No. 20 (page 145)?

6.4   Would data-directed input/output have any advantage over the list-directed input/output used in Example No. 13 (page 107)?

6.5   Write a PL/I program which reads 51-character groups from the input file. The first character of each group will be the letter A, B, C, D, or E; the next 50 characters will be digits. There will be no blanks between groups, or within a group. The program should perform the following operations, based on the first character:

First Character	Treat the remaining 50 characters as ...
A	Five 10-digit integers, assigning them to elements 2, 4, 6, 8, and 10 of a fixed-point array named A1.
B	Ten 5-digit integers, assigning them to the first ten elements of A1.
C	Ten floating-point numbers of precision (5, 2), assigning them to the first ten elements of a floating-point array named A2.
D	Ignore; process the next 51-character group.
E	Ignore; terminate the program.

CHAPTER 7

PROCEDURES

A procedure in PL/I is a set of statements designed to accomplish some particular objective. Each of the program examples used in this book so far has consisted of a single procedure; the objective of each procedure has been identical to the objective of the whole program. The objective of a program as a whole is called the main objective; it is a result of executing the main program.

In general, some intermediate results must be obtained during the execution of a main program. These intermediate results are then used to obtain other intermediate results and so on, until the main results are obtained. Intermediate results may be obtained directly, by statements in the main program, or they may be obtained by other programs - subordinate to the main program - which are executed as required. Such sub-programs, because they consist of PL/I statements designed to accomplish some particular objective, are also procedures.

The general structure of a PL/I program as a whole
thus consists of two kinds of procedures: a single main procedure, and any number (including zero) of subprograms,
each of which is also a procedure. The main procedure is
identified by the option MAIN, as in the program examples.

Every PL/I program must contain at least one procedure
with the MAIN option.* This procedure may "call" other procedures - subprograms - in the course of execution, and the
subprograms may call other subprograms. Calling a subprogram amounts to transferring control to it, suspending execution of the calling program. When the subprogram has completed its work it "returns" to the calling program, which then
resumes execution. Usually, but not necessarily, the subprogram will have performed some operations, the results of
which are needed by the calling program when control is returned
to it. A subprogram may be called as many times, from as
many places, as required; it will normally return to the calling
program at the point following the statement which called it.

For an example of a program using a subprogram, we
will discuss a program which reads three numbers corresponding

---

* If more than one procedure has the MAIN option, the first one
encountered during compilation is taken as the main program.

to the three dimensions of a rectangular box and computes the length of the diagonal of the box. We can think of the box as having height H, width W, and depth D, as shown in the illustration below. Given values for these dimensions, the program is to calculate the length of the diagonal, E.

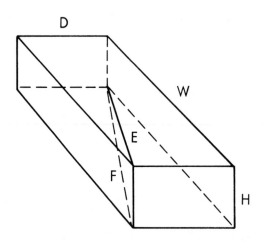

In order to calculate the length of the diagonal, E, we must first calculate the length of the face diagonal, F. The length of F can be determined from the values of W and D by the Pythagorean Theorem:

$$F = \sqrt{W^2 + D^2} \ .$$

The length of E can then be determined, also by the Pythagorean Theorem:

$$E = \sqrt{F^2 + H^2} \ .$$

To solve the problem (in principle) we need only apply the Pythagorean Theorem twice. If we write a subprogram to apply the Pythagorean Theorem, then we need only call the subprogram twice; we do not have to write the necessary PL/I statements each time.

For purposes of writing the subprogram, we will assume that the Pythagorean Theorem means taking the square root of the sum of the squares of two quantities which we will call parameters, which are called SIDE1 and SIDE2. This is the subprogram:

```
HYPOT:    PROCEDURE( SIDE1, SIDE2 ) FLOAT ;
              /* COMPUTE HYPOTENUSE OF RIGHT TRIANGLE
                 GIVEN TWO SIDES. */
              DECLARE ( SIDE1, SIDE2 ) FLOAT ;
              RETURN( SQRT( SIDE1**2 + SIDE2**2 ) ) ;
          END HYPOT ;
```

The above sequence of statements declares the identifier HYPOT to be the name of a procedure, the function of which is to compute the square root of the sum of the squares of two quantities and return the result to the calling program. The two quantities, SIDE1 and SIDE2 are the parameters to HYPOT.

Parameters to a procedure are enclosed in parentheses to the right of the word PROCEDURE, and are separated by commas.

The attribute FLOAT in the first line specifies that the value returned by HYPOT is to be a floating-point number.

The DECLARE statement serves its usual purpose, to define the attributes of variables used in the program. In this case, the only variables are the parameters.

The RETURN statement specifies the value that HYPOT is to return to the calling program. In this case, it specifies that the value is to be the square root of the sum of the squares of the two parameters.

The complete program to solve the original problem - computing the length of the diagonal of a box - is shown on the following page. The first executable statement in the program is the GET statement labeled START. The statements in procedure HYPOT are compiled, but they are not executed until the two statements following the GET statement are executed. In other words, the statement

```
HYPOT:    PROCEDURE( SIDE1 , SIDE2 ) FLOAT ;
```

tells the compiler three things:

1.   Subsequent statements constitute a declaration

     of a procedure named HYPOT;

2.   The procedure has two parameters; and

3.   The procedure will return a floating-point value.

```
DIAG: PROCEDURE OPTIONS (MAIN) ;

        /* EXAMPLE NO. 28
           READ THREE SIDES OF A BOX AND COMPUTE THE
           LENGTH OF THE DIAGONAL. */

        DECLARE ( H, W, D, E, F ) FLOAT ;

        HYPOT:   PROCEDURE( SIDE1, SIDE2 ) FLOAT ;

                    /* COMPUTE HYPOTENUSE OF RIGHT
                       TRIANGLE GIVEN TWO SIDES. */

                    DECLARE ( SIDE1, SIDE2 ) FLOAT ;

                    RETURN( SQRT( SIDE1**2 + SIDE2**2 ) ) ;
                 END HYPOT ;

START:    /* MAIN PROGRAM STARTS HERE. */
          GET DATA( H, W, D ) ;

          /* COMPUTE DIAGONAL ON FACE. */
          F = HYPOT( W, D ) ;

          /* COMPUTE DIAGONAL. */
          E = HYPOT( F, H ) ;

          /* PRINT DATA AND RESULTS. */
          PUT DATA( H, W, D, E ) ;

          GO TO START ;
       END DIAG ;
```

The statement

$$F = HYPOT(W, D) ;$$

specifies that the subprogram HYPOT is to be executed, using the values of the variables W and D. These identifiers are called <u>actual parameters</u>, or <u>arguments</u>; they have a one-for-one correspondence to the <u>parameters</u>, or <u>formal parameters</u>, used in the procedure declaration. The above statement is identical to

$$F = SQRT(W**2 + D**2) ;$$

The relationship of actual and formal parameters is fundamental to the concept of subprograms. The actual parameters - used when a subprogram is called - are in effect substituted for the formal parameters. Consequently, <u>it is very important that the attributes of actual parameters be the same as those of the corresponding formal parameters.</u>

The names of formal parameters are unimportant, but they must be identifiers. Formal parameters have absolutely no relation to any other identifiers in a program, outside of the procedure declaration in which they appear. Consequently,

their names can be chosen independently of names chosen for

use elsewhere in a program.

Actual parameters can pass values to procedures, receive

values from procedures, and, in the case of parametric labels,

serve as destinations for transfer statements in procedures.

The formal parameters specify how the actual parameters are

to be used when a procedure is called. The following procedure

illustrates all three kinds of parameters:

```
QUAD: PROCEDURE( X, Y, Z, R1, R2, ERROR ) ;

          /* EXAMPLE NO. 29
             SOLVE QUADRATIC EQUATION, GIVEN COEFFICIENTS
             X, Y, AND Z. RESULTS ARE RETURNED IN R1 AND R2.
             TRANSFER TO 'ERROR' IF X=0 OR DISCRIMINANT<0. */

          DECLARE ( X, Y, Z, R1, R2 ) FLOAT, ERROR LABEL,
                  ( DISC, DENOM ) FLOAT ;

          IF X=0 THEN GO TO ERROR ;

          DISC = Y**2 - 4*X*Z ;
          IF DISC<0 THEN GO TO ERROR ;

          DISC = SQRT( DISC ) ;
          DENOM = X + X ;
          R1 = ( -Y + DISC ) / DENOM ;
          R2 = ( -Y - DISC ) / DENOM ;
          RETURN ;
      END QUAD ;
```

When procedure QUAD (Example No. 29) is called, the actual parameters corresponding to X, Y, and Z will pass values to it. The actual parameters corresponding to R1 and R2 will receive values from it. In the event of an error, QUAD will transfer to the actual parameter corresponding to ERROR, which must be a statement label.

The parameters X, Y, and Z, and their corresponding actual parameters, are sometimes called "value" parameters because their values are important to the procedure. The parameters R1, R2, and ERROR, and their corresponding actual parameters are sometimes called "name" parameters because their names, i.e., their locations in the computer, are important to the procedure.

A fundamental difference between procedure QUAD and procedure HYPOT, which was discussed previously, is that HYPOT itself effectively takes on a value, but QUAD does not. Instead, QUAD merely calculates two values and places them into the actual parameters corresponding to R1 and R2. A procedure like HYPOT, which itself takes on a value, is called a function procedure, or simply, a function. A procedure like QUAD, which does not itself take on a value, is called a subroutine procedure, or simply, a subroutine. Functions are called by using their names in expressions, e.g.,

$$F = HYPOT(W, D) ;$$

Subroutines are called by the CALL statement, which has the general form

$$CALL \ procedure \ (\ actual \ parameters \ ) ;$$

where

procedure is the name of the subroutine procedure being called, and

actual parameters are the actual parameters, or arguments.

The following program example uses the subroutine QUAD to solve ten quadratic equations with coefficients in arrays A, B, and C. The roots of each equation are placed in the corresponding elements of two other arrays, ROOT1 and ROOT2. If any set of coefficients results in an error the appropriate elements of ROOT1 and ROOT2 are set to zero and an informative message is printed.

211

```
SOLVE:    PROCEDURE OPTIONS (MAIN) ;

              /* EXAMPLE NO. 30
                 SOLVE TEN SETS OF QUADRATIC EQUATIONS. */

              DECLARE ( A, B, C, ROOT1, ROOT2 )(10) FLOAT,
                      I  FIXED ;

QUAD: PROCEDURE( X, Y, Z, R1, R2, ERROR ) ;

              /* EXAMPLE NO. 29
                 SOLVE QUADRATIC EQUATION, GIVEN COEFFICIENTS
                 X, Y, AND Z. RESULTS ARE RETURNED IN R1 AND R2.
                 TRANSFER TO 'ERROR' IF X=0 OR DISCRIMINANT<0. */

              DECLARE ( X, Y, Z, R1, R2 ) FLOAT, ERROR LABEL,
                      ( DISC, DENOM ) FLOAT ;

              IF X=0 THEN GO TO ERROR ;

              DISC = Y**2 - 4*X*Z ;
              IF DISC<0 THEN GO TO ERROR ;

              DISC = SQRT( DISC ) ;
              DENOM = X + X ;
              R1 = ( -Y + DISC ) / DENOM ;
              R2 = ( -Y - DISC ) / DENOM ;
              RETURN ;
          END QUAD ;

              /* READ INPUT DATA */
              GET LIST( A, B, C ) ;

     L:      DO I = 1 BY 1 TO 10 ;
                  CALL QUAD( A(I), B(I), C(I), ROOT1(I),
                             ROOT2(I), ERR ) ;
                  GO TO NORMAL ;
     ERR:         ROOT1(I), ROOT2(I) = 0 ;
                  PUT SKIP LIST ('ERROR, EQUATION', I,
                                 'COEFFICIENTS =',
                                 A(I), B(I), C(I)) ;
   NORMAL:   END L ;

              PUT LIST( (A(I), B(I), C(I), ROOT1(I), ROOT2(I)
                      DO I = 1 TO 10) ) ;

          END SOLVE ;
```

The form of the RETURN statements in a procedure determine whether it is a function or a subroutine. If they are of the form

$$\text{RETURN(} \underline{\text{expression}} \text{) ;}$$

the procedure is a function; its value is that of the expression. If the RETURN statements consist of the single word RETURN, the procedure is a subroutine.

Functions must always contain at least one RETURN statement, since by definition they return a value to the calling program. Subroutines return to the calling program either by executing a RETURN statement, or by executing the END statement. (Thus, the RETURN statement in subroutine QUAD is redundant.) There is no restriction on the maximum number of RETURN statements that may appear in a function or in a subroutine.

A single procedure can have the properties of a function and a subroutine at the same time. That is, it can modify the actual parameters and at the same time take on a value itself. For example, subroutine QUAD can be modified to take on a value of 1 or 0 if an equation is or is not solved correctly:

```
QUAD2:    PROCEDURE( X, Y, Z, R1, R2 ) FLOAT ;

              /* EXAMPLE NO. 31
                 SOLVE QUADRATIC EQUATION, GIVEN COEFFICIENTS
                 X, Y, AND Z. RESULTS ARE RETURNED IN R1 AND R2.
                 QUAD2 TAKES ON VALUE 0 IF X=0 OR DISCRIMINANT
                 <0, ELSE 1. */

              DECLARE ( X, Y, Z, R1, R2 ) FLOAT,
                      ( DISC, DENOM ) FLOAT ;

              IF X=0 THEN RETURN( 0 ) ;

              DISC = Y**2 - 4*X*Z ;
              IF DISC<0 THEN RETURN( 0 ) ;

              DISC = SQRT( DISC ) ;
              DENOM = X + X ;
              R1 = ( -Y + DISC ) / DENOM ;
              R2 = ( -Y - DISC ) / DENOM ;
              RETURN( 1 ) ;
          END QUAD2 ;
```

The essence of Example No. 30 could then be reduced to

```
DO I = 1 BY 1 TO 10 ;
   IF   QUAD2( A(I), B(I), C(I), ROOT1(I), ROOT2(I) )=0
        THEN  ROOT1(I), ROOT2(I) = 0 ;
END ;
```

QUAD2 could also be called by means of a CALL statement, but there would be no way of knowing if an error occurred.

When a procedure works with the value of an actual
parameter, rather than its name, the actual parameter can be
an expression. The statements

$$F = \text{HYPOT}(\ W, \ D \ ) \ ;$$

$$E = \text{HYPOT}(\ F, \ H \ ) \ ;$$

could be combined into a single statement:

$$E = \text{HYPOT}(\ \text{HYPOT}(\ W, \ D \ ), \ H \ ) \ ;$$

That is, the value yielded by HYPOT(W, D) is used as one of the two arguments (the other is H) in a second call of HYPOT.

Arrays can be passed as arguments to procedures, provided, as usual, that the attributes of the arrays are the same as the attributes of the corresponding formal parameters. The following procedure could be used in a checker-playing program to determine the number of checkers remaining on the board:

```
CHK_BD:   PROCEDURE( BOARD, REDS, BLACKS ) ;

          /* EXAMPLE NO. 32
             DETERMINE NUMBER OF CHECKERS ON A CHECKERBOARD.
             RED CHECKERS ARE REPRESENTED BY +1, BLACKS BY -1.
             UNOCCUPIED SQUARES CONTAIN 0. */

          DECLARE ( BOARD(8,8), REDS, BLACKS ) FIXED,
                  ( I, J ) FIXED ;

          REDS, BLACKS = 0 ;

          DO I = 1 BY 1 TO 8 ;
             DO J = 1 BY 1 TO 8 ;
                IF BOARD(I,J)=1 THEN REDS = REDS + 1 ;
                IF BOARD(I,J)=-1 THEN BLACKS = BLACKS + 1 ;
          END CHK_BD ;
```

When CHK_BD is called during execution of the checker-playing program, the first argument must be the name of a fixed-point array declared with the dimension attribute (8, 8). The second and third arguments must be fixed-point simple variables. All of the arguments must be of default precision, because no precision attribute is specified in the declaration for the formal parameters.

When structures are passed as actual parameters to procedures, there are several ways in which they can be treated by the procedures. The program example below calls two procedures, UPDATE and LISTER (declarations for which are not shown). How would the corresponding formal parameters

```
CK_ACC:   PROCEDURE OPTIONS (MAIN) ;
                 /* EXAMPLE NO. 33
                    UPDATE CHECKING ACCOUNTS, USING OTHER SUBPRO-
                    GRAMS FOR THE UPDATE AND OUTPUT FUNCTIONS. */

                 DECLARE   1 ACCOUNT,
                           2 NAME,
                           (3 LAST,
                            3 FIRST)     CHARACTER(12),
                            3 MIDDLE     CHARACTER(3),
                           2 NUMBER      FIXED,
                           (2 OLD_BAL,
                            2 SER_CHG,
                            2 NEW_BAL)   FLOAT ;

                 GET LIST (ACCOUNT) ;
                 CALL UPDATE( ACCOUNT ) ;
                 CALL LISTER( NAME, NUMBER ) ;
           END CK_ACC ;
```

be declared in the declarations for UPDATE and LISTER? One

way would be to declare the formal parameters in the same way

as the actual parameters, i.e., for UPDATE:

```
UPDATE:   PROCEDURE( STRUCT ) ;
              DECLARE 1 STRUCT,
                     2 MINOR,
                     (3 ELEM_1,
                      3 ELEM_2)   CHARACTER(12),
                      3 ELEM_3    CHARACTER(3),
                     2 ELEM_4     FIXED,
                     (2 ELEM_5,
                      2 ELEM_6,
                      2 ELEM_7)   FLOAT ;
              .
              .
              .
```

For LISTER:

```
LISTER:   PROCEDURE( STRUCT, NUM ) ;
              DECLARE 1 STRUCT,
                     (2 ELEM_1,
                      2 ELEM_2)   CHARACTER(12),
                      2 ELEM_3    CHARACTER(3),

              NUM FIXED ;
              .
              .
              .
```

All of the elementary items in the DECLARE statement in

LISTER are on level 2, but they could have been declared to be

on some other level, e.g., 3, without altering the structuring

of the formal parameter STRUCT. The DECLARE statement

would still declare STRUCT to be the name of a structure having

217

three elementary items with the indicated attributes. The

corresponding actual parameter must therefore be the name of

a structure having three elementary items with the corresponding

attributes. In Example No. 33, the actual parameter is NAME,

which is a structure having the required characteristics.

On the other hand, the called procedure might need to

use the actual parameter as a minor structure. The declaration

for UPDATE might begin:

```
UPDATE:   PROCEDURE( CHECKING ) ;

              DECLARE   1 MAJOR,
                          2 CHECKING,
                            3 NAME,
                            (4 LAST,
                             4 FIRST)      CHARACTER(12),
                             4 MIDDLE      CHARACTER(2),
                            3 NUMBER       FIXED,
                            (3 OLD_BAL,
                             3 SER_CHG,
                             3 NEW_BAL)    FLOAT,
                          2 SAVE,
                            3 NAME,
                            (4 LAST,
                             4 FIRST)      CHARACTER(12),
                             4 MIDDLE      CHARACTER(2),
                            3 NUMBER       FIXED,
                            (3 OLD_BAL,
                             3 DIVIDEND,
                             3 NEW_BAL)    FLOAT ;
                  .
                  .
                  .
              END UPDATE ;
```

The formal parameter, CHECKING, has the same struc-

turing as the actual parameter, ACCOUNT, in Example No. 33.

It is essential that the attributes of actual parameters be the same as those of the corresponding formal parameters, but it is not always easy to meet this requirement. In order to get around the difficulty, we can use the ENTRY attribute to specify the attributes of actual parameters; the parameters will be converted automatically whenever necessary. The general form of the ENTRY attribute as included in a DECLARE statement is

DECLARE name ENTRY(att, att, ..., att) ;

where

name is a function or subroutine name, and

att are the attributes of the respective formal parameters, i.e., the required attributes of the actual parameters.

The ENTRY declaration for procedure QUAD (page 209) would be

DECLARE QUAD ENTRY(FLOAT, FLOAT, FLOAT, FLOAT, FLOAT, LABEL) ;

and would be included in Example No. 30 (page 212), for instance, with the declarations for A, B, C, etc.

When a parameter is an array, the notation in the ENTRY attribute is one or more asterisks (one for each dimension) separated by commas and enclosed in parentheses. The state-

ment

```
DECLARE   PROC   ENTRY( (*,*,*) FIXED, (*) CHARACTER(10) ) ;
```

declares PROC to be a procedure; the first parameter is a

three-dimensional fixed-point array, and the second is a one-

dimensional array of character strings of length 10.

When a parameter is a structure, the notation in the

ENTRY attribute is a list of level numbers separated by commas.

Attributes may be appended to elementary level numbers, but

may not be factored. The first level number for each param-

eter must be 1. The statement

```
DECLARE   P2   ENTRY( 1, 2 FLOAT, 2, 3 FIXED, 3 FIXED, FLOAT ) ;
```

declares P2 to be a procedure; the first parameter is a struc-

ture which can be visualized as

1 A,

   2 B FLOAT,

   2 C,

     3 D FIXED,

     3 E FIXED

The statement also specifies that the second parameter to P2 is a floating-point variable of default precision.

It is also essential that the values returned by functions have the attributes expected by the calling program. The RETURNS attribute is used to specify the attributes of function values; the values will be converted automatically to the attributes required by the calling program. The general form of the RETURNS attribute as included in a DECLARE statement is

DECLARE name ENTRY(attributes)

RETURNS(attributes) ;

The ENTRY declaration for procedure HYPOT (page 205) would be

```
DECLARE HYPOT ENTRY( FLOAT, FLOAT ) RETURNS( FLOAT ) ;
```

and would be included in Example No. 28 (page 207), for instance, with the declarations for H, W, D, E, and F.

If a function name is not declared with the RETURNS attribute, the compiler assumes the default attributes apply to the name. We strongly recommend that you specify the attributes of function names by means of the ENTRY and RETURNS attributes. For essentially the same reason, we strongly recommend that you specify the attributes of function and subroutine parameters by means of the ENTRY attribute.

Is there any relationship between identifiers used in a procedure and identifiers used elsewhere in a program? In the case of formal parameters, there is <u>no</u> relationship, even if the program uses identifiers spelled in exactly the same way outside of the procedure. However, other identifiers used in a procedure may be identical to the same identifiers used outside the procedure. The rule is

> Identifiers appearing as formal parameters or in a DECLARE statement in a procedure have <u>no</u> relationship to any identifiers used outside of the procedure.

The corollary rule is

> Identifiers, other than formal parameters, which do not appear in a DECLARE statement in a procedure <u>are identical to the same identifiers used outside of the procedure.</u>

In order to understand the meaning of these rules, consider the following construction:

```
P1:    PROCEDURE OPTIONS (MAIN) ;
               DECLARE   A   FIXED INITIAL( 3 ) ;
               P2:    PROCEDURE ;
                          DECLARE   A   FIXED INITIAL( 10 ) ;
                          P3:    PROCEDURE ;
③                                    PUT LIST( A ) ;
                                 END P3 ;
②                        CALL P3 ;
④                        PUT LIST( A ) ;
                     END P2 ;
①             CALL P2 ;
⑤             PUT LIST( A ) ;
          END P1 ;
```

The numbers to the left of the executable statements in the above construction show the sequence in which they are executed. The first executable statement calls procedure P2, which immediately calls P3.

The PUT statement in procedure P3 prints the value of the variable named A. This "A" is the same "A" that is used in P2, the containing procedure, because the identifier does not appear in a DECLARE statement in P3. The printed value will be 10.

Procedure P3 returns to the PUT statement (④) in P2, the calling program. Since the "A" in P3 is identical to the "A" in P2, the printed value will again be 10.

Procedure P2 returns to the PUT statement (⑤) in P1, the calling program. However, the value printed by that statement will be 3. Because A is declared in P2, it has no relation to the variable of the same name in P1. The "A"s in P1 and P2 are entirely unrelated.

The variable named A declared in P1 is said to be known throughout P1, exclusive of P2. That variable is not known in P2 because another variable of the same name is declared there. This latter variable is known throughout P2, inclusive of P3, because it is not redeclared there. Conversely, the "A" declared in P2 is not known in P1. It is said to be local to P2, and global to P3. In general, the areas in which an identifier is known are called the scope of the identifier.

The appearance of an identifier in a DECLARE statement defines that identifier to be local to the procedure in which it is declared. Consequently, its attributes may be different in different declarations. For example, in the construction

```
P1:    PROCEDURE ;
          DECLARE  XYZ  FIXED ;
       P2:    PROCEDURE ;
                 DECLARE   XYZ   BIT(1) ;
              P3:    PROCEDURE ;
                        DECLARE   XYZ   FLOAT ;
                          .
                          .
                          .
                      END P3 ;
                   .
                   .
                END P2 ;
             .
             .
          END P1 ;
```

the identifier XYZ is a fixed-point variable in P1, exclusive of
P2; a bit string of length 1 in P2, exclusive of P3; and a floating-
point variable in P3.

The rules governing the scopes of identifiers can be modified by the EXTERNAL attribute which specifies that identifiers
in a procedure are to be identical to the same identifiers in other
procedures. In the following illustration the identifier ABC refers
to the same variable in procedures P1 and P3. A separate variable
having the name ABC is local to P2, and yet another is local to P4.

225

```
P1:    PROCEDURE ;
            DECLARE  ABC  FIXED EXTERNAL ;
       P2:    PROCEDURE ;
                 DECLARE  ABC  FLOAT ;
            P3:    PROCEDURE
                      DECLARE  ABC  FIXED EXTERNAL ;
                 P4:    PROCEDURE ;
                           DECLARE  ABC  FLOAT ;
                      END P4 ;
                 END P3 ;
            END P2 ;
       END P1 ;
```

When the EXTERNAL attribute is given to an identifier, any other attributes specified must be consistent with other EXTERNAL declarations for the identifier.

Procedures need not be nested in precisely the way they have been in the examples presented up to this point. The rule for nesting procedures is equivalent to the rule for nesting DO loops: if a procedure is begun within another procedure, it must be terminated within the same procedure. Illustration (a) on the following page is a diagram of a properly constructed PL/I program. Illustration (b) shows a construction which is improper because it violates the nesting rule.

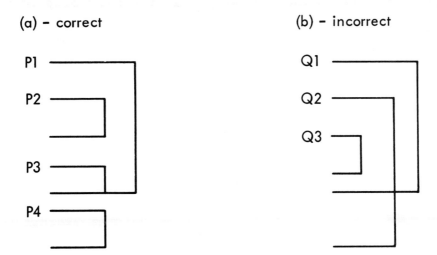

(a) – correct   (b) – incorrect

P1   Q1

P2   Q2

      Q3

P3

P4

If illustration (a) is assumed to represent an entire PL/I program, then P1 and P4 are called <u>external</u> procedures. Any identifiers declared with the EXTERNAL attribute in both P1 and P4 are identical. Thus, the EXTERNAL attribute can be used to establish communication between external procedures as well as between an internal procedure and the outermost procedure of a nest.

Any PL/I program comprises a collection of external procedures. One of these procedures must have the option MAIN which identifies it as the procedure in which execution is to begin. The MAIN option may not be used with an internal procedure.

The procedures constituting a program may appear in

any sequence. Thus, the following is a valid PL/I program:

```
PX:     PROCEDURE ;
          .
          .
        CALL PZ ;
          .
          .
        END PX ;
PY:     PROCEDURE OPTIONS (MAIN) ;
          .
          .
        CALL PZ ;
          .
          .
        CALL PX ;
          .
          .
        END PY ;
PZ:     PROCEDURE ;
          .
          .
        END PZ ;
```

As implied in the illustration above, procedure names are implicitly EXTERNAL. Thus, PY (the main program) can call PZ and PX; PZ can call PX; and PX can call PZ. In general, any external procedure can call any other external procedure. However, no procedure may call the main procedure.

The ability to construct PL/I programs by collecting external procedures is a very definite advantage. Any procedure which uses only local identifiers and formal parameters, if any, can in principle be added to the collection; the only changes required to the main program would be the addition of CALL statements or function references as appropriate.

Procedure QUAD (page 209) could be incorporated into any PL/I program to provide the facility for solving quadratic equations. In order to use the facility, it is necessary to know only

1. the procedure name (QUAD),

2. that the first three arguments are the coefficients,

3. that the next two arguments will be given the values of the roots, and

4. that the last argument is a label to which QUAD will transfer upon detecting an error.

If an ENTRY declaration is not used, then it is also necessary to know the attributes of the formal parameters to QUAD so that it can be called with the proper actual parameters.

Procedure QUAD is perfectly general; it can, with no modification whatsoever, be included in any PL/I program which must solve a quadratic equation. Any procedure which uses only local identifiers and formal parameters, if any, possesses the same generality. Use of such procedures for purposes which are fairly common, yet difficult to program, e.g., solution of a large set of simultaneous equations, can greatly reduce the amount of time and effort required to write programs. Sometimes, such use makes the construction of a program that would

otherwise be impossible very simple. For example, linear programming is a very useful technique for finding the optimum
solution to problems with many interrelated variables where
some of the relationships may be very complicated. An individual with extensive knowledge of linear programming techniques
could write a procedure which someone with much less knowledge
could then use to solve his problem. Such a procedure could be
written once and stored in a "program library" where it would be
available to anyone having need of it.

Notes on Chapter 7

1.   In order to minimize the chances for error, the attributes
        of parameters to a procedure should be specified in two
        places:

            in an ENTRY declaration contained in the procedure
            which calls it, and

            in a DECLARE statement within the procedure itself.

        For function procedures, the attributes of the result
        returned should likewise be specified in two places:

            in a RETURNS attribute appended to the associated
            ENTRY declaration, and

in the PROCEDURE statement itself, following the
parameter list.

2.   A procedure may call itself; the process is called <u>recur-</u>

<u>sion.</u> If a procedure is to be recursive, it must have the

RECURSIVE attribute, as illustrated below, and there must

be some provision for terminating the recursion. The

procedure below computes the factorial of its argument.

(The factorial of a number is the product of the integers

from 1 to the number.)

```
FACT: PROCEDURE( N ) RECURSIVE FIXED ;

      /* EXAMPLE NO. 34
         THIS PROCEDURE TAKES ON THE VALUE OF
         N-FACTORIAL. */

      DECLARE N FIXED ;

      IF N<=1 THEN RETURN( 00001 ) ;
      ELSE RETURN( N*FACT( N-1 ) ) ;
      END FACT ;
```

EXERCISES

7.1   Rewrite Exercise 4.4 as a generalized matrix multiplication subroutine called by the statement

$$\text{CALL MMULT(} \underline{a}, \underline{b}, \underline{c} \text{) ;}$$

where $\underline{a}$, $\underline{b}$, and $\underline{c}$ are two-dimensional arrays having
bounds (1:15) in each dimension.

7.2   Write a "driver" program that will call MMULT to test
it. Include an ENTRY declaration for MMULT.

7.3   Write a non-recursive function to compute factorials. Is
your function more, or less, efficient than Example No. 34
on page 231?

7.4   Write a function that evaluates polynomials of the form

$$a_0 + a_1x + a_2x^2 + \dots a_nx^n$$

and which is called by the expression

$$\text{POLY(A, N, X)}$$

where

A is a one-dimensional array having a lower subscript
bound of zero,

N is the degree of the polynomial (N<20), and

X is the value of the variable.

Write a driver program to test your function using several

polynomials and several values of the variable for each.

7.5 Write a subroutine which accepts the array of structures

ACCOUNT shown in Example No. 20 (page 145) and sorts

the contents into ascending order by account number.

CHAPTER 8

BLOCK STRUCTURE

Any PL/I program consists of one or more external procedures, each of which can contain "local" and "global" identifiers. Internal procedures, i.e., procedures contained within
other procedures, may also contain local and global identifiers.

A program segment which can contain local identifiers is
called a <u>block</u>. Two kinds of blocks are provided for in PL/I:
procedure blocks, described in the preceding chapter; and
BEGIN blocks, described in this chapter. The term "block"
refers to either kind of block and the context indicates which
kind is meant.

The general form of a BEGIN block is

BEGIN ;

statement(s) ;

END ;

BEGIN blocks are entered in the normal sequence of execution, as contrasted with procedure blocks which are entered by means of CALL statements or function references. Consequently, a BEGIN block must be contained within another block, which may be either another BEGIN block or a procedure block. The outermost block must, of course, be an external procedure.

The concept of "scope of identifiers" applies to BEGIN blocks in exactly the same way as it applies to procedure blocks. However, BEGIN blocks cannot have parameters, so the rules become

1. Any identifiers declared within a block are local to the block.

2. Any identifiers not declared within a block are global to the block.

The EXTERNAL attribute can be used to modify the second rule, as described in Chapter 7.

One of the most useful properties of blocks is that they can give a "dynamic" character to programs. That is, they can be used to establish various program characteristics during execution, rather than during compilation. A typical application is the allocation of storage for arrays. For instance, one of the previous program examples using arrays contained the statement

```
              DECLARE ( A, B, C )(10) FLOAT ;
```

to declare three arrays, each having ten elements. The amount

of data placed into these arrays may require fewer than ten

elements, in which case the DECLARE statement is wasteful

of space in storage. The maximum amount of data that can be

accommodated is limited to ten items in each array; if more

must be accommodated, the DECLARE statement must be

rewritten to allocate more storage. In general, it is impossible

to write declarations which allocate sufficient space for arrays,

yet do not allocate excessive space.

Suppose a program is to read a set of numbers into an

array. If the set is preceded by an integer telling how many

numbers there are in the set, part of the program might be

```
        P1:    PROCEDURE OPTIONS (MAIN) ;
               DECLARE   A(100)    FLOAT,
                         (I, N)    FIXED ;
               GET LIST( N, (A(I) DO I = 1 TO N) ) ;
               .
               .
               .
        END P1 ;
```

If the value of N is less than 100, the array declaration is

wasteful of storage. If N is greater than 100, an error will occur. Both possibilities can be avoided by reading a value for

N and then allocating storage for the array. This can be done

easily by using a BEGIN block; the program becomes

```
P2:    PROCEDURE OPTIONS (MAIN) ;
           DECLARE  N  FIXED ;
           GET LIST( N ) ;
           BEGIN ;
              DECLARE  A(N)  FLOAT ;
              GET LIST( A ) ;
                 .
                 .
                 .
           END ;
              .
              .
              .
       END P2 ;
```

Storage for the array A in the above program excerpt is

allocated when the BEGIN block is entered. The number of

elements allocated is the value of N, a variable which is global

to the block. It is important to note that the value of N must

have been established prior to entry into the block, i.e., before

the array A is declared. It would be useless to place the GET

statement ahead of the DECLARE statement for A in the same

block because, as stated in Chapter 2, blocks are scanned for

DECLARE statements and attributes are established before the

executable statements are compiled. In one sense, DECLARE
statements are also executable: they allocate storage and assign
attributes. In this sense, they are always the first statements
to be executed when a block is entered, regardless of their
physical placement within a block.

The following example illustrates the use of a BEGIN block
in a complete PL/I program:

```
SUMLIST: PROCEDURE OPTIONS (MAIN) ;

        /* EXAMPLE NO. 35
           READ LISTS OF NUMBERS INTO AN ARRAY, ADD THEM, AND
           PRINT THE TOTAL OF THE ITEMS IN EACH LIST. LISTS
           MAY BE OF VARYING LENGTH; ALLOCATE JUST ENOUGH
           STORAGE TO ACCOMMODATE THE PARTICULAR LIST IN
           PROCESS. */

        DECLARE ( I, N ) FIXED ;

START:   GET LIST( N ) ; /* NUMBER OF ITEMS IN NEXT LIST. */

        BEGIN ;
           DECLARE A(N) FLOAT,
                   TOTAL FLOAT INITIAL(0) ;

           GET LIST( (A(I) DO I = 1 TO N) ) ;
           DO I = 1 TO N ;
              TOTAL = TOTAL + A(I) ;
           END ;

           PUT LIST( N, TOTAL ) ;
        END ;

        GO TO START ;

     END SUMLIST ;
```

The DECLARE statement in the BEGIN block causes the array A and the variable TOTAL to be defined anew each time the block is entered. TOTAL is initialized to zero each time storage is allocated for it.

BEGIN blocks may be entered only in the normal course of program execution, and procedure blocks may be entered only as a result of CALL statements and function references. It is an error to attempt to transfer to the interior of a block from a point outside the block. The arrows in the diagram below represent permissible transfers; transfers in the opposite direction are not permissible.

The arrows in the diagram also apply to procedure calls: a procedure may not be called from a point outside the block in which it is contained. External procedures, of course, may be called from any point in a program.

When an identifier is used in a block, the block is checked to determine if the identifier is declared in that block. If not,

the next outer block is checked, and so on, until the identifier
is found to be defined or until the outermost block (an external
procedure) is checked. If the identifier is not defined it is
given the default attributes if it is a data item, or is in error
if it is a label. The abbreviated program below shows how
identifiers are interpreted:

```
P:  PROCEDURE OPTIONS (MAIN) ;
        .
     A:  BEGIN ;
            .
         B:  BEGIN ;
                .
             L1:     GO TO L2 ;
                .
             C:  BEGIN ;
                    .
                 GO TO L1 ;
                    .
                 GO TO L2 ;
                    .
             L2:  END C ;
         END B ;
            .
     L?:  END A ;
     END P ;
```

The GO TO statement near the beginning of block B
transfers control to the statement labeled L2 in block <u>A</u>. The
first GO TO statement in block C transfers control to the statement labeled L1 in block B. The second GO TO statement in
block C transfers control to the statement labeled L2 in block
<u>C</u>, i.e., to the END statement for block C.

The preceding example illustrates two other characteristics of blocks:

1. A label on a BEGIN statement, i.e., the name of a block, is global to the block which is begun by the statement.

2. A label on an END statement is local to the block which is ended by the statement.

In the illustration below, the identifier Y is known within block X and within block Y, assuming it is not redefined there. The identifier YX is known only within block Y.

```
X: BEGIN ;
        .
        .
    Y: BEGIN ;
            .
            .
        YX: END Y ;
        .
        .
    END X ;
```

Block Y could be entered from any point in block X by means of the statement GO TO Y. Once control is transferred to Y it would normally proceed in sequence from that point, returning to block X at the first statement following the END statement labeled YX.

The principal advantage of blocks is that they permit programs to make the most efficient use of storage. Storage is allocated upon entry to a block, and freed upon exit; the space that is used in one block may be used for some other purpose in another block. For instance, a program might need to use an array with the dimension attribute (50, 50) during the earlier phases, and an array with the dimension attribute (2500) during some later phases. Both arrays have 2500 elements, but it is not necessary to allocate 5000 elements if both arrays need not be available at the same time. The program would be organized like this:

```
P: PROCEDURE OPTIONS (MAIN) ;
        BEGIN ;
           DECLARE   A(50,50) ;
              •
              •
              •
        END ;
        BEGIN ;
           DECLARE   B(2500) ;
              •
              •
              •
        END ;
     END P ;
```

Any storage areas that are required in both blocks would be declared in a DECLARE statement preceding the first block.

Note on Chapter 8

A certain amount of time is required to perform allocation, initialization, and other functions upon block entry. Therefore, it is preferable to declare as much storage as possible in outer blocks, and as little as possible in inner blocks.

EXERCISES

8.1 Write a subroutine that mutliplies two square matrices and is called by the statement:

CALL MMULT(A, B, C, N) ;

where A and B are the matrices to be mutliplied, C is the resulting matrix, and N is the size of each of the three matrices.

CHAPTER 9

PROGRAM INTERRUPTIONS

Once a program has been compiled, it may not execute correctly. Some errors can be traced to errors in program logic, or "bugs," and some can be traced to faulty data. Bugs can be eliminated through the process of "debugging," but errors due to faulty data can occur even in bug-free programs.

Often, a bug or a data error will give rise to a condition which can be detected by the program. Some of the more common conditions which usually indicate an error are listed below. Other conditions (some of which may not indicate errors) are given in Appendix D.

Condition	Meaning
OVERFLOW	A floating-point quantity has become too large to be represented in the computer.
UNDERFLOW	A floating-point number has become too small (in magnitude to be represented in the computer.

FIXEDOVERFLOW	A fixed-point number has become too large to be represented in the computer.
ZERODIVIDE	The expression used as the denominator has the value zero, leading to an undefined operation.
SUBSCRIPTRANGE	The value of an expression used as a subscript has a value outside of the bounds declared for an array.
ENDFILE	There are no more data in the standard input file.

When a condition is raised, it causes the PL/I program to be interrupted while control is transferred to a special program called the operating system.* The operating system analyzes the cause of the interrupt and then performs a "standard system action" which depends on the condition that caused it.

It is frequently very useful to specify, by means of PL/I statements, actions to be taken in lieu of the standard system action for various conditions. The specification is accomplished by means of the ON statement, which has the general form

ON condition on-unit ;

---

* Also known as the monitor, supervisor, or control program.

246

where

condition is the name of a condition, e.g., ENDFILE, and

on-unit is a PL/I statement (other than a DO statement),
or a BEGIN block.

The unit associated with an ON statement is not executed

at the time the ON statement is executed; it is executed when and

if the specified condition subsequently arises.

The program example below uses an ON statement for the

FIXEDOVERFLOW condition in order to accomplish its purpose:

to determine the largest binary integer that can be stored in the

particular computer on which the program is executed.

```
LARGEST: PROCEDURE OPTIONS (MAIN) ;

               /* EXAMPLE NO. 36
                  DETERMINE THE LARGEST INTEGER THAT CAN BE
                  CONTAINED IN THE COMPUTER, ASSUMING THAT
                  INTEGER IS OF THE FORM 2**N-1 (A VALID
                  ASSUMPTION FOR MOST COMPUTERS). */

               DECLARE NUMBER BINARY FIXED INITIAL( 1 ) ;

               ON FIXEDOVERFLOW GO TO FOUND ;
DOUBLE:        NUMBER = NUMBER + NUMBER ;
               GO TO DOUBLE ;

FOUND:         NUMBER = NUMBER + ( NUMBER - 1 ) ;
               PUT LIST( NUMBER ) ;
           END LARGEST ;
```

In Example No. 36, the value of NUMBER is added to itself repeatedly. At some point the expression

NUMBER + NUMBER

will give a result that is greater than the largest number that can be contained in the computer, and the attempted addition will raise the FIXEDOVERFLOW condition. The condition will be raised before the assignment operation is performed and control will be transferred immediately to the appropriate on-unit. This unit is a GO TO statement which transfers control to the label FOUND.

The assignment statement labeled FOUND produces a number of the form 2^n-1, consistent with the assumption mentioned in the comment. You can verify this by assuming that the largest number is 7, for example, and working through the calculations just as the computer would.

What would happen if the ON statement were removed from Example No. 36? The fixed-point overflow condition would still be raised, but the action taken would be the standard system action. The standard action differs for various conditions, but two things usually happen: a message is printed to inform you

that the condition arose, and then either execution is terminated
or it resumes - perhaps with data which became invalid as a
result of the condition.

In some cases, it may be desirable to specify an action to
be taken when, for example, the FIXEDOVERFLOW condition is
raised in one part of a program, and a different action if it is
raised in another part of the program. This is easily done by
writing another ON statement:

```
          .
          .
          .
ON FIXEDOVERFLOW GO TO BIGA ;
          .
          .
          .
ON FIXEDOVERFLOW GO TO BIGB ;
          .
          .
          .
```

The second ON statement completely overrides the first.
Any fixed-point overflow occurring in statements between the
two ON statements will cause the program to transfer to the
statement labeled BIGA. Any fixed-point overflow occurring
after the second ON statement has been executed will cause a
transfer to the statement labeled BIGB.

When ON statements appear in nested blocks, they do not

necessarily override ON statements that were executed previously. For example, in this construction

```
A: BEGIN ;
       .
       .
   ON FIXEDOVERFLOW GO TO BIGA ;
       .
       .
   B: BEGIN ;
          .
          .
      ON FIXEDOVERFLOW GO TO BIGB ;
          .
          .
      BIGB:
          .
          .
       END B ;
       .
       .
   BIGA:
       .
       .
 END A ;
```

any fixed-point overflow condition arising prior to execution of the first ON statement will result in standard system action. The first ON statement, when it is executed, establishes the statement GO TO BIGA as the on-unit for the FIXEDOVERFLOW condition. This unit remains in effect as execution proceeds into block B until the ON unit in that block is executed. At that time, the effective on-unit for the FIXEDOVERFLOW condition becomes the statement GO TO BIGB.

What happens when control passes out of block B? The statement GO TO BIGA is re-established as the on-unit for the

FIXEDOVERFLOW condition. In other words, when the ON statement in block B is executed, the on-unit GO TO BIGA is temporarily suspended; the unit GO TO BIGB is "stacked" on it. When control leaves block B, the unit GO TO BIGA is restored. On-units can thus be redefined in much the same way that identifiers can be redefined by DECLARE statements in nested blocks.

An on-unit may specify that no action is to be taken if a condition is raised, i.e., that the condition is to be ignored. This is accomplished simply by using a null statement as the on-unit.

Once an on-unit has been established for a condition, it may be canceled in two ways. One way is to execute an ON statement with the word SYSTEM as the on-unit. SYSTEM specifies that the standard system action is to be taken if the associated condition is subsequently raised. (At the start of execution the operating system establishes SYSTEM as the on-unit for every possible condition.)

The second way to cancel an on-unit is to execute a REVERT statement, which has the general form

REVERT condition ;

Execution of a REVERT statement within a block causes execution to proceed as though no ON statement for the specified condition had been executed in the same block. If the statement

REVERT FIXEDOVERFLOW ;

had been executed in block B in the illustration on page 250 after the ON statement in that block had been executed, the effect would have been to restore the on-unit GO TO BIGA.

In order to investigate conditions more closely, recall that programs are executed under the control of the operating system. The diagram below illustrates the general way in which conditions are processed. The diagram is not a flow chart in the usual sense, because it does not represent a program; instead, it represents a sequential process.

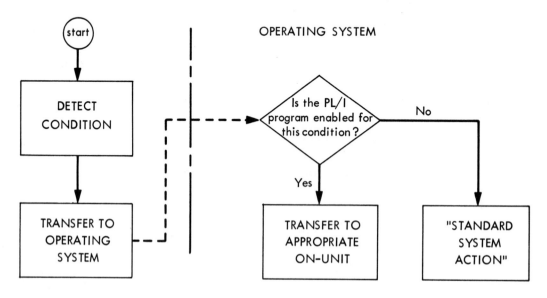

The first two steps in processing a condition are first, to detect its existence; and second, to transfer control to the operating system. There are two distinct ways in which these steps can be accomplished. One way is for the computer circuits to detect the existence of a condition and automatically signal the operating system. Conditions that can be detected in this way are called <u>initially enabled</u> conditions. The other way is for the PL/I program to detect the existence of a condition by means of programmed tests and transfer to the operating system if appropriate. Conditions that must be detected in this way are called <u>initially disabled</u> conditions. Thus, on any computer there are two classes of conditions: those that are initially enabled, and those that are initially disabled. The specific conditions in each class may differ among various computers.

In order to enable conditions that are initially disabled, the compiler must generate the appropriate instructions when it is compiling the program. Inclusion of these instructions is specified by means of <u>prefixes</u> associated with particular statements or blocks. The general form of a prefix is

$$(\underline{condition_1}, \underline{condition_2}, \dots) : \underline{unit} ;$$

where each <u>condition</u> is the name of a condition to be enabled, and <u>unit</u> is a statement, a procedure, or a BEGIN block. Each condition is enabled for the duration of execution of the associated unit.

Assuming that SUBSCRIPTRANGE is initially disabled, the on-unit in the illustration below will not be executed, despite the fact that the subscript obviously takes on values outside the permissible range. The instructions necessary to detect the condition will not be generated by the compiler, so the condition will not be detected during execution.

```
ANOMALY: PROCEDURE OPTIONS (MAIN) ;

         DECLARE   A(-3:3) FLOAT,
                   I    FIXED ;

         ON SUBSCRIPTRANGE PUT LIST( I ) ;
LOOP:    DO I = -5 BY 1 TO 5 ;
             A(I) = 0 ;
         END LOOP ;
             .
             .
         END ANOMALY ;
```

In order to detect the error (by raising the SUBSCRIPTRANGE condition), the first line in the above illustration must be changed to read

```
(SUBSCRIPTRANGE): ANOMALY:   PROCEDURE OPTIONS (MAIN) ;
```

254

It is not necessary to use an ON statement for conditions
that are enabled by prefixes. As long as a condition is enabled,
whether it is initially enabled, or is enabled by its appearance in
a prefix, there is an associated standard system action. An ON
statement would be used only if the standard action is not satisfactory. The standard actions for various conditions are given
in Appendix D.

Just as disabled conditions can be enabled by prefixes,
enabled conditions can be disabled by prefixes. To disable a
condition, the condition is written in a prefix preceded by NO.
Assuming that FIXEDOVERFLOW is enabled, the on-unit in the
illustration below can be executed as a result of statements L1
and L3, but not as a result of L2.

```
INHIBIT: PROCEDURE OPTIONS (MAIN) ;
            DECLARE ( A, B, C ) FIXED ;
            ON FIXEDOVERFLOW GO TO ERROR ;
            .
            .
            .
   L1:      A = B + C ;
            .
            .
            .
   (NOFIXEDOVERFLOW): L2:
            B = A + C ;
            .
            .
            .
   L3:      C = A + B ;
            .
            .
            .
         END INHIBIT ;
```

255

Although conditions such as OVERFLOW can be processed to recover from contingencies during execution, they are not usually very helpful when you are trying to find logical errors. Logical errors can usually be located by inspecting the PL/I source program and the results, but sometimes it may be necessary to monitor the sequence in which the program is executed. The CHECK condition provides a simple way of monitoring execution: it can be used to indicate each change in the value of a variable, each execution of a labeled statement, and each procedure call.

The CHECK condition is initially disabled, and must, therefore, be enabled by means of a prefix. Further, the particular identifiers to be checked must be specified so that the compiler can generate the appropriate instructions to check each one. The general form of the prefix enabling the CHECK condition is

(CHECK(identifier list)) :

where identifier list is a list of variables, unsubscripted array names, structure names, procedure names, and/or labels.

The standard system action for the CHECK condition depends on the kind of identifier for which the condition is raised. For variables, the standard action is to print the name of the variable followed by the value; for labels, the standard action is to print the label and a count of the number of times the associated statement has been executed. Similar information is printed for the other kinds of identifiers for which the condition can be raised. In the following example, an informative message will be printed each time the variable I and the array A (any element) take on new values; and each time the statement labeled L is executed.

```
CHECKIT: PROCEDURE OPTIONS (MAIN) ;
            /* EXAMPLE NO. 37
               MONITOR EXECUTION. */

            DECLARE ( A(10), I ) FIXED ;
            A = 0 ;

(CHECK( A, I, L )): B:
            BEGIN ;
    LAB:        DO I = 1 BY 1 TO 10 ;
    L:              A(I) = 3*I ;
            END LAB ;
        END B ;
        END CHECKIT ;
```

The CHECK condition should be enabled as infrequently as possible, and for as few identifiers as are absolutely necessary. The condition can easily result in a great deal of output, which may be more confusing than helpful. Usually, a great deal of information can be obtained by enabling the CHECK condition until it has been raised a certain number of times for a particular identifier, and then disabling it by means of a REVERT statement. Another way is to enable the CHECK condition and then specify a non-standard action which does not cause printing until the condition has been raised a certain number of times. The following program illustrates the principle: no CHECK-output is printed for the variable I until its value has been changed three times; no CHECK-output is printed for the label L until the associated statement has been executed three times.

```
LIM_CK:   PROCEDURE OPTIONS (MAIN) ;
               /* EXAMPLE NO. 38
                  HYPOTHETICAL PROGRAM TO ILLUSTRATE LIMITED
                  CHECKING. */

               DECLARE ( I, ICOUNT, LCOUNT ) FIXED INITIAL( 0 ) ;
(CHECK( I, L )): B:
               BEGIN ;
                  ON CHECK( I ) ICOUNT = ICOUNT + 1 ;
                  ON CHECK( L ) LCOUNT = LCOUNT + 1 ;
      LA:        DO I = 1 BY 1 TO 10 ;
      L:             PUT LIST( I ) ;
                     IF ICOUNT=3 THEN REVERT CHECK (I) ;
                     IF LCOUNT=3 THEN REVERT CHECK (L) ;
                  END LA ;
               END B ;
            END LIM_CK ;
```

Sometimes, during program checkout, it is useful to "simulate" various conditions that may arise in order to verify that the program reacts to them in the proper way. Conditions are raised by the SIGNAL statement, which has the general form

SIGNAL condition ;

where condition is the name of the condition to be raised. The effect of the statement

```
L:   SIGNAL FIXEDOVERFLOW ;
```

is precisely the effect that would occur had a fixed-point overflow occurred in the statement labeled L. If the statement were used in a program to simulate an overflow condition, then it would be re- placed by the actual statement required at L after the program had been checked out.

The ON and SIGNAL statements can be used in conjunction with each other to monitor program execution. An ON statement can specify a "programmer-defined" condition, and a SIGNAL statement can be used to raise the condition. Programmer-defined conditions are arbitrary identifiers, and have no relation to the conditions described previously. The general form of corres- ponding ON and SIGNAL statements for a programmer-defined condition are

ON CONDITION (<u>identifier</u>) <u>on-unit</u> ;

and

SIGNAL CONDITION (<u>identifier</u>) ;

The ON, REVERT, and SIGNAL statements are very useful for tracking down elusive program bugs. As you gain experience in programming you will also gain experience in debugging, and will find that you will be able to use these statements to great advantage in getting good results back from the computer.

These statements have many uses aside from debugging. A complete list of conditions is given in Appendix D; many of them can be used to simplify and generalize your programs. For instance, the ENDFILE condition makes it relatively simple to write a program which will read and process data from a file of unknown length.

EXERCISES

9.1   What is the effective on-unit for OVERFLOW in each of
these programs at the time the statement labeled X is
executed?

```
P1:        PROCEDURE OPTIONS (MAIN) ;
              ON OVERFLOW GO TO Y ;
Y:             •
               •
               •
           ON OVERFLOW GO TO Z ;
           BEGIN ;
              ON OVERFLOW ;
                •
              REVERT OVERFLOW ;
                •
              REVERT OVERFLOW ;
                •
           END ;
X:             •
               •
               •
Z:         END P1 ;
```

```
P2:        PROCEDURE OPTIONS (MAIN) ;
              ON OVERFLOW GO TO Y ;
Y:             •
               •
           BEGIN ;
              ON OVERFLOW SYSTEM ;
                •
                •
                •
           END ;
X:             •
               •
               •
           END P2 ;
```

261

CHAPTER 10

CHARACTER MANIPULATION

All of the uses of computers discussed so far in this book have been concerned with the processing of arithmetic data. That is, in most cases, we have read numbers into the computer and used these numbers to calculate other numbers; the final results have been numbers. In some cases, we have carried alphabetic (character string) data along with the computations, but we have not performed any operations on them.

PL/I contains a number of facilities for processing string data, i.e., non-numeric data. In this chapter, we will be concerned exclusively with character strings, but the same principles apply to bit strings.

One of the characteristics of any string is its length, i.e., how many characters it contains. The character string 'COMPUTER' has a length of 8, and we can think of it as appearing in the computer as

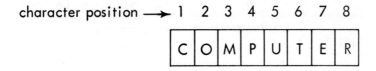

character position ⟶ 1 2 3 4 5 6 7 8

| C | O | M | P | U | T | E | R |

Each character in the string has a unique position, noted by a number. Position number 1 is the leftmost character.

String data can be assigned to string variables by means of the familiar assignment statement. The program example below illustrates a few string assignment statements.

```
ASSIGN:  PROCEDURE OPTIONS (MAIN) ;

         /* EXAMPLE NO. 39
            STRING ASSIGNMENT */

         DECLARE   STRING_1   CHARACTER(8),
                   STRING_2   CHARACTER(10),
                   STRING_3   CHARACTER(5) ;

         STRING_1 = 'COMPUTER' ;
         STRING_2 = STRING_1 ;
         STRING_3 = STRING_2 ;

         PUT EDIT( STRING_1, STRING_2, STRING_3 )
                 ( SKIP, A ) ;

         END ASSIGN ;
```

The DECLARE statement allocates space for three strings. We can visualize these strings as in the following illustration. Initially, the contents of each character position is undefined.

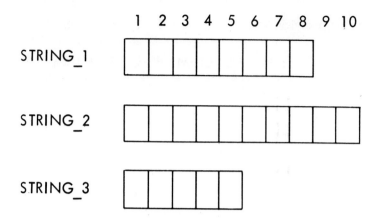

STRING_1

STRING_2

STRING_3

The first assignment statement in Example No. 39 places the string COMPUTER into STRING_1. The contents of each character position in STRING_1 is now defined, namely:

1 2 3 4 5 6 7 8

STRING_1 | C | O | M | P | U | T | E | R |

The second assignment statement transfers the contents of STRING_1 to STRING_2, which can then be thought of as containing

1 2 3 4 5 6 7 8 9 10

STRING_2 | C | O | M | P | U | T | E | R | | |

What are the contents of positions 9 and 10 of STRING_2 after the assignment statement is executed? The answer is, blanks. STRING_2 is longer (10 positions) than STRING_1

264

(8 positions). The rule is

> When a shorter string is assigned to a variable
> which is the name of a longer string the string
> is filled out to the right with blanks.*
>
> Note: The character "b" will be used in this
> chapter to represent a blank.

We can now visualize the assignment statement

$$STRING\_2 = STRING\_1 ;$$

by the illustration

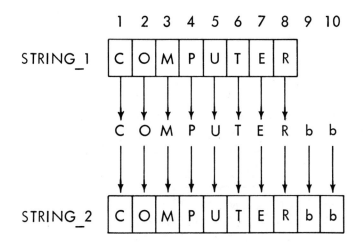

The contents of STRING_2 would have been the same if

the assignment statement had been

$$STRING\_2 = 'COMPUTER' ;$$

---

* The process of adding characters to make a data item assume
a specified length is called padding. In PL/I, the padding
character for character strings is the blank.

The third assignment statement in Example No. 39 transfers the contents of STRING_2 to STRING_3. However, the length of STRING_3 is only 5 characters. The rule in this case is

> When a longer string is assigned to a variable which is the name of a shorter string the string is truncated on the right.

We can now visualize the assignment statement

$$STRING\_3 = STRING\_2 ;$$

by the illustration

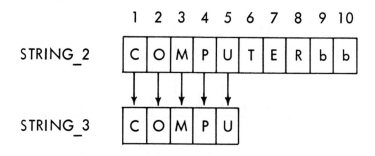

In general, a string assignment statement has the form

destination string = source string ;

which means, simply, that characters are transferred from the source string to the destination string. The number of characters transferred depends entirely on the length of the destination string:

> If the lengths of the destination and source strings are equal, the strings will be identical after the assignment.
>
> If the length of the destination string exceeds that of the source string, blanks are added to the right of the source characters.
>
> If the length of the destination string is less than that of the source string, the excessive characters on the right are ignored.

Suppose, now, that we want to perform the following operation:

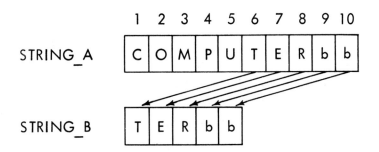

That is, STRING_A is the source string and STRING_B is the destination string, but instead of beginning the transfer with the first character of STRING_A we want to begin with the sixth character. In other words, we want to replace STRING_B with a substring of STRING_A.

Substrings are specified in PL/I by the built-in function
SUBSTR, which has two general forms. One of them is

SUBSTR(string, position) ;

where

string is a character string, and

position is an arithmetic expression.

The PL/I statement to perform the operation on the preceding page would be

STRING_B = SUBSTR(STRING_A, 6) ;

which states, "beginning with character 6 of STRING_A, transfer characters to STRING_B." As usual, blanks will be added if
STRING_B is longer than the substring of STRING_A; the substring will be truncated if STRING_B is shorter.

The second form of SUBSTR allows us to specify the number of characters to be transferred, in addition to specifying the
starting character position. This form is

SUBSTR(string, position, nchars) ;

where nchars is an arithmetic expression specifying the number of characters to be transferred.

The following example illustrates some of the things that can be done with SUBSTR.

```
PLAY: PROCEDURE OPTIONS (MAIN) ;

        /* EXAMPLE NO. 40
           ILLUSTRATE THE SUBSTR FUNCTION */

        DECLARE WORD CHARACTER(8) INITIAL( 'COMPUTER' ),
                LETTER(8) CHARACTER(1),
                LETTERV(8) CHARACTER(8),
                Q FIXED ;
    L:      DO Q = 1 BY 1 TO 8 ;
               LETTER(Q) = SUBSTR( WORD, Q, 1 ) ;
               LETTERV(Q) = SUBSTR( WORD, 1, Q ) ;
            END L ;

        PUT EDIT( (LETTER(Q),LETTERV(Q) DO Q = 1 TO 8) )
                ( SKIP, 2A(10) ) ;
        END PLAY ;
```

Initially, the character string variable WORD has the following contents:

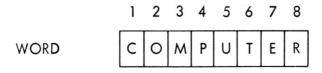

At the time the PUT statement is executed the two arrays have the contents illustrated on the following page. That is, the Qth element of LETTER contains the Qth character of WORD. The Qth element of LETTERV contains the first Q characters of WORD.

269

	LETTER	LETTERV
(1)	C	C b b bb bbb
(2)	O	CO b bb bbb
(3)	M	COMb bbbb
(4)	P	COMPb bbb
(5)	U	COMPU bbb
(6)	T	COMPUTbb
(7)	E	COMPUTEb
(8)	R	COMPUTER

The SUBSTR function can also be used to specify a sub-string of the destination string, i.e., it may be used to the left of the = in an assignment statement.* Example No. 41 on the following page places a character string into an array in the same way Example No. 40 placed a string into the array LETTER (see above), and then reconstructs the string in another character string variable.

---

* When so used, SUBSTR is called a pseudo-variable because it specifies the destination in an assignment operation, but SUBSTR itself - the function - is not the destination.

```
PLAY_1:   PROCEDURE OPTIONS (MAIN) ;

               /* EXAMPLE NO. 41
                  BREAK A STRING INTO INDIVIDUAL CHARACTERS,
                  PLACING ONE CHARACTER INTO EACH ELEMENT OF
                  AN ARRAY. THEN RECONSTRUCT THE WORD. */

               DECLARE ( OLD_WORD, NEW_WORD ) CHARACTER(8),
                          LETTER(8)  CHARACTER(1),
                          Q   FIXED ;

               OLD_WORD = 'COMPUTER' ;

               /* DECOMPOSE THE WORD. */
     L:        DO Q = 1 BY 1 TO 8 ;
                  LETTER(Q) = SUBSTR( OLD_WORD, Q, 1 ) ;
               END L ;

               /* RECONSTRUCT THE WORD IN NEW_WORD. */
     L2:       DO Q = 1 BY 1 TO 8 ;
                  SUBSTR( NEW_WORD, Q, 1 ) = LETTER(Q) ;
               END L2 ;

               PUT LIST( OLD_WORD, NEW_WORD ) ;
           END PLAY_1 ;
```

The SUBSTR function, as we have seen, can be used to
break strings apart in various ways, and can also be used to
put them together. Another way to build a string is to add
characters to the end of it by the process of <u>concatenation.</u>
The concatenation operator, ||, read "concatenated with,"
operates in the following way:

    'A' || 'B'   yields   'AB'

    'T' || 'H' || 'E'   yields   'THE'

271

The following example uses concatenation to pluralize
words by adding the character "S".

```
PLURAL:   PROCEDURE OPTIONS (MAIN) ;

                /* EXAMPLE NO. 42
                   READ A WORD, ADD THE CHARACTER 'S', AND
                   PRINT THE RESULT. */

                DECLARE  WORD  CHARACTER(20) VARYING ;

START:          GET LIST( WORD ) ;
                WORD = WORD || 'S' ;
                PUT LIST( WORD ) SKIP ;
                GO TO START ;

           END PLURAL ;
```

The identifier WORD in the above example has the

VARYING attribute. One reason for this is that the words

read in may be of differing lengths. The primary reason,

however, is that concatenation itself - by definition - changes

the length of a string. The strings being concatenated may be

of fixed lengths, but as a general rule, the destination string

should be of varying length.

Suppose we have a string of characters and it is desired

to know where a certain substring, e.g., 'ABC', appears in

the string. We could examine the string using the SUBSTR

function and several IF statements, but that would make for a

rather complicated program. Problems of this nature arise

frequently, especially in the discipline of information retrieval, and so PL/I contains a built-in function, INDEX, to simplify the process of finding the desired substring.

The INDEX function has the general form

INDEX(string, argument) ;

where

string is the string to be examined, and

argument is the desired substring. In the vocabulary of information retrieval, this argument is called the search argument.

The value of the INDEX function is the character position in the string of the leftmost character of the substring represented by the search argument. If the argument does not occur in the string, the value of INDEX is zero. If it occurs more than once, the value of INDEX is the position of its first occurrence.

To illustrate the use of INDEX, assume we have a string named ALPHABET of length 26, containing the alphabet in the usual sequence. Then the following statements will have the indicated results:

273

```
P = INDEX( ALPHABET, 'XYZ' ) ;                    P is set to 24
P = INDEX( ALPHABET, 'E' ) ;                          "         5
P = INDEX( ALPHABET, 'EF' ) ;                         "         5
P = INDEX( ALPHABET, 'AZ' ) ;                         "         0
```

The SUBSTR function can be combined with the INDEX function to give added character-handling facilities to PL/I programs. Example No. 43 on the following page reads a sentence and counts the frequency of appearance of each letter.

The variable named SEARCH is used in Example No. 43 for two reasons. First, it is used to reduce the amount of computation required in the inner loop. Second, it simplifies the statements which reference INDEX.

The facilities for manipulating characters permit use of the computer in many non-numeric applications. Typical applications include text-editing and justification, language translation, and composition of music. Some of the following exercises indicate typical applications of non-numeric uses of computers.

```
FREQ: PROCEDURE OPTIONS (MAIN) ;

          /* EXAMPLE NO. 43
             READ A SENTENCE AND PREPARE A FREQUENCY TABLE
             OF THE LETTERS IT CONTAINS. */

          DECLARE ALPHABET  CHARACTER(26)  INITIAL
                            ('ABCDEFGHIJKLMNOPQRSTUVWXYZ'),
                  SENTENCE  CHARACTER(100) VARYING,
                  SEARCH  CHARACTER(1),
                  ( FREQUENCY, P, P1, Q ) FIXED ;

START:    /* READ THE SENTENCE */
          GET LIST( SENTENCE ) COPY ;

   L1:    DO Q = 1 BY 1 TO 26 ;

             /* ESTABLISH THE SEARCH ARGUMENT AS THE
                Q'TH LETTER OF THE ALPHABET. */
             SEARCH = SUBSTR( ALPHABET, Q, 1 ) ;

             /* INITIALIZE OCCURRENCES OF ARGUMENT */
             FREQUENCY = 0 ;

             /* FIND FIRST OCCURRENCE OF ARGUMENT */
             P1, P = INDEX( SENTENCE, SEARCH ) ;

             /* FIND REST OF OCCURRENCES */
   L2:       DO WHILE ( P¬=0 ) ;
                /* THIS LOOP IS VACUOUS IF THE ARGUMENT
                   DOES NOT OCCUR AT ALL, AS P IS 0 */

                FREQUENCY = FREQUENCY + 1 ;
                P = INDEX(SUBSTR(SENTENCE,P1+1), SEARCH) ;
                P1 = P1 + P ;
             END L2 ;

             /* PRINT ARGUMENT AND NUMBER OF OCCURRENCES. */
             PUT LIST( SUBSTR(ALPHABET, Q, 1 ), '=',
                       FREQUENCY ) SKIP ;
          END L1 ;

          GO TO START ;

       END FREQ ;
```

EXERCISES

10.1 Read a character string of arbitrary length (not more than 20 characters) and reverse the order of the characters. (Use the LENGTH function to determine the length of the string.) For example, if the input string is ABC, the output string should be CBA.

10.2 Read a character string of arbitrary length (not more than 100 characters) and print the first non-blank character. Assume the string includes at least one non-blank character.

10.3 Read a character string of arbitrary length (not more than 200 characters). Delete all blanks and print the resulting condensed string.

10.4 Read a character string of arbitrary length (not more than 200 characters), representing text. Print out those words which begin with "A".

10.5 Read a character string of arbitrary length (not more than 200 characters), representing text. Print

1. The number of sentences in the text.

2. The average number of words in a sentence.

3. The average number of letters per word.

10.6 Read a character string of arbitrary length (not more than 200 characters) representing a sentence. Convert each word to Pig Latin by the following rule:

Move all characters preceding the first vowel to the end of the word and append "AY".

Print the resulting sentence, including the terminal period.

CHAPTER 11

ADDITIONAL INPUT/OUTPUT FACILITIES

Computers, as we have discussed them so far, have for the most part operated on internal data, with input/output operations being almost incidental to the total operation. In many applications, the opposite relationship is the case: input/output operations predominate, while the internal processing plays a relatively minor part. There is no fundamental difference in the language used, but some additional considerations become important when input/output is a primary concern.

When input/output is a relatively minor concern the "standard" files can usually be used for input and output; all that is needed is one input file, and one output file. When input/output is the primary concern, however, the reason is usually that there are large quantities of data to be processed. The input data may exist in several input files, and it may be desirable to route output data to several output files.

278

Whenever it is inappropriate to use the standard files, we can use files to which we have given specific names. A name is declared to be a file by means of the FILE attribute in a DECLARE statement:

DECLARE name FILE ;

The effect of the FILE attribute is to associate name (which must of course be an identifier) with an external device, such as a magnetic tape unit, a typewriter, or a printer. The particular external device with which a name is associated must also be specified (perhaps outside the PL/I program), but the way in which this is done varies among computer installations. The important thing is that a file name refers to a single external device, and when we specify the name in a GET or PUT statement, as shown below, we are stating that data are to be read from or written on a particular file, i.e., a specific input/output device.

When the standard input file is used, a typical GET statement might be

GET LIST(A, B, C) ;

When a non-standard file is used, the statement becomes

GET FILE(name) LIST(A, B, C);

where name has been declared with the FILE attribute. A non-standard file is specified in a PUT statement in the same way as for a GET statement, e.g.,

PUT FILE(name) EDIT(list) (format) ;

As you know, the standard output file is equivalent to a printer, but a non-standard output file is not necessarily equivalent to a printer. To make a name refer to a printer, it must have the PRINT attribute as well as the FILE attribute:

DECLARE name FILE PRINT ;

(where the attributes FILE and PRINT need not appear in that order). If a file does not have the PRINT attribute, the options SKIP, LINE, PAGE, and COLUMN are meaningless.

Depending on the device with which it is associated, a file may be an input file, an output file, or an input/output file. (See the table on page 158). If a file name is associated with an output device, it may appear only in a PUT statement; if it is

associated with an input/output device, it may appear in GET
and/or PUT statements.

We can specify in a file declaration how the file is to be
used, namely, as an input file, an output file, or an input/
output file. Unless specified as an input or an output file, a
file is assumed to be an input/output file. A file function is
specified by the INPUT or OUTPUT attribute in a DECLARE
statement, e. g. ,

DECLARE name FILE INPUT ;

(where the attributes FILE and INPUT need not appear in the
order shown). The PRINT attribute mentioned on the preceding
page applies only to output files, and may not be used in combination with the INPUT attribute. It may be used in combination
with the OUTPUT attribute, in which case OUTPUT is redundant.

The association of a particular file name to a particular
device may (depending on the computer installation) be made
outside the PL/I program, independently of any attributes
specified for the name in a DECLARE statement in the program.
That is, the attributes specified for a file name do not force
the association of the name with any particular kind of device.

Since the attributes might be specified independently of the actual association with a physical device, it is very important to make sure that the device actually associated with a file name is consistent with the attributes specified for it.

The term "file" in the present context is in many ways similar to a file such as you might find in an office. In an office, before information can be filed or extracted, the file must first be opened. In PL/I, files can be opened by the first input/output statement that references them. Files opened in this way are said to be opened <u>implicitly</u>. The operating system performs the opening operation before the input/output statement is executed.

In an office, once a file has been used, it may be closed or may be left open. The PL/I files we have used so far have been opened implicitly by the first input/output statement that referenced them, and have been left open for the remainder of program execution. They have been closed (implicitly) at the end of execution.

PL/I files can be opened and closed <u>explicitly</u> by means of the OPEN and CLOSE statements, respectively. These statements have the general form

$$\text{OPEN FILE(} \underline{\text{name}} \text{) ;}$$

and

$$\text{CLOSE FILE(} \underline{\text{name}} \text{) ;}$$

When we open a file, we can specify the purpose for which we are opening it: input or output. After using it for the specified purpose, we can close the file, and then open it again for some other purpose. The following example takes three numbers from the standard input file, writes them in another file, and then reads them back from that file into different variables.

```
INOUT:    PROCEDURE OPTIONS (MAIN) ;
             /* EXAMPLE NO. 44
                READ THREE NUMBERS FROM STANDARD INPUT FILE,
                WRITE THEM ON TEMPORARY FILE, READ THEM BACK
                FROM THE TEMPORARY FILE INTO DIFFERENT
                VARIABLES. */

             DECLARE ( X, Y, Z, A, B, C ) FLOAT,
                     TEMP   FILE ;

             GET LIST( X, Y, Z ) ;

             OPEN FILE( TEMP ) OUTPUT ;
             PUT FILE( TEMP ) LIST( X, Y, Z ) ;
             CLOSE FILE( TEMP ) ;

             OPEN FILE( TEMP ) INPUT ;
             GET FILE( TEMP ) LIST( A, B, C ) ;

             PUT LIST( A, B, C ) SKIP ;

          END INOUT ;
```

The most important things to note about Example No. 44 are:

The physical device associated with TEMP must be an input/output device.

No attributes (other than the FILE attribute) are included in the declaration for TEMP, because it is used both as an input and as an output file.

TEMP can be referenced only in PUT statements during the time it is open as an output file and only by GET statements during the time it is open as an input file.

No input/output statements may refer to TEMP during the time it is closed, i.e., between the CLOSE statement and the subsequent OPEN statement.

The CLOSE statement has the effect of repositioning TEMP so that the first data item to be read after TEMP has been reopened is the first data item in the file.

One final thing to note about files is that if an output file associated with an input/output device is closed and then opened again as an output file, any data subsequently written in that file will destroy the data previously placed there. In other words, when a file associated with an input/output device is closed, it is repositioned to the beginning; any subsequent input/output operations (after the file is reopened) will either re-read or re-write the first data item(s). In the latter case, the data previously in the file will be destroyed.

In practice, the first data item in a file associated with an input/output device is sometimes a special item, called a header label, and the last item is also a special item, called a trailer label. These labels serve to identify the structure and contents of the file. File identification labels are written and read by means of the IDENT option on OPEN statements. A label may be written only on an output file and read from an input file. The general forms of the OPEN statement with the IDENT option are:

OPEN FILE(name) INPUT IDENT(string) ;

OPEN FILE(name) OUTPUT IDENT(expression) ;

where

string is the name of a character string variable, and

expression is either a character string variable or a character string constant.

Where an input file is opened by an OPEN statement with the IDENT option, the header label is placed into the character string variable specified in the IDENT option. The variable can then be compared to the desired label to make sure that the file

associated with <u>name</u> is the right one. For example, a payroll

program might maintain salaries in a file which has the header

label SALARIES; the program expects to find this information on

the physical device associated with the file INPUT_1. The

following statements could be used to make sure that the proper

data are contained in the file on the external device associated

with the file name INPUT_1.

```
DECLARE INPUT_1 FILE INPUT,
        HEADER CHARACTER(100) VARYING ;
  .
  .
  .
OPEN FILE( INPUT_1 ) INPUT IDENT( HEADER ) ;
IF HEADER-='SALARIES'  THEN GO TO ERROR ;
  .
  .
  .
```

The reason for using a 100-character varying length

string for the variable HEADER is that if an incorrect file is

used, the label might exceed the eight characters expected.

Also, if the file has no label at all, the result is the null string.

(This fact again points out that labels are distinguishable from

data.)

When an output file is opened by an OPEN statement with
the IDENT option, the characters in the expression are placed
in the file as the header label for the file.

Suppose a company wants to update its salary records.
The existing records are assumed to be in file OLD_SAL, and
the updated records are to be placed in the file NEW_SAL. The
header label for NEW_SAL should include the date on which the
file was written. If the proper label for the old file is
'SALARIES AS OF 6/30/66', and the label for the new file is
to be 'SALARIES AS OF 7/31/66', part of the update program
might be as follows:

```
SAL_ADJ: PROCEDURE OPTIONS (MAIN) ;

         /* XYZ COMPANY - UPDATE SALARIES */

         DECLARE   OLD_SAL   FILE INPUT,
                   NEW_SAL   FILE OUTPUT,
                   HEADER    CHARACTER(100) VARYING ;

         OPEN FILE( OLD_SAL ) IDENT( HEADER ) ;
         IF HEADER¬='SALARIES AS OF 6/30/66' THEN
            DO ;
               PUT LIST( 'WRONG FILE ON OLD_SAL' ) SKIP ;
               GO TO STOP ;
            END ;

         OPEN FILE( NEW_SAL )
            IDENT( 'SALARIES AS OF 7/31/66' ) ;
            .
            .
            .
STOP: END SAL_ADJ ;
```

The IDENT option may be used with the CLOSE statement in the same way as it is used with the OPEN statement, except that trailer, instead of header, labels are involved. The operations performed to close a file depend on whether the file is (or was opened as) an input file or an output file; they are the same as any IDENT operations performed when the file was last opened.

By this time, you should have a pretty good idea of what files are, and how they can be used. Let us now look more closely at what happens when we read information into the computer from a file and write information into a file from the computer.

If we execute the statement:

GET FILE(name) LIST(A) ;

the data item (singular, assuming A is a simple variable) is not transmitted directly from the file into the computer memory location corresponding to A. Instead, it is brought from the file into another area of computer memory, called a buffer, and is then transferred from the buffer to the location corresponding to A. Any data conversion necessary is performed during the transfer from the buffer to A; not during transmission from the file to the buffer. Data input is thus a two-step opera- tion: from the file to a buffer, and from the buffer to the desti- nation. Only the file and the destination are specified in a GET statement; the operating system establishes and controls the buffer automatically. Data output is similarly a two-step operation.

There is one buffer for each <u>open</u> file; there is no buffer associated with a <u>closed</u> file. (This is why input/output state- ments cannot be used with closed files.)

When a buffer is first established, that is, when the associated file is opened, the buffer is empty. The first GET statement to be executed (which may be the same statement that opened the file) causes data to be brought into the buffer from the associated physical device. However, the amount of data brought in is determined by the size of the buffer, and not by the GET statement. The data are brought into the buffer without conversion, meaning, in the case of list-directed input for example, that all blanks between data items are brought in along with the data items themselves. Transmission stops when the buffer is full, or an end-of-file is sensed. In the latter event, a special character might be set into the buffer to mark the position of the end-of-file, or the position of the last data item in the buffer might be noted by the operating system.

After the buffer has been filled, it is scanned for data. The scan commences at the first location in the buffer. For list- and data-directed input, if the first location contains a blank, the scan proceeds to the next location, continuing until a data item is found. The scan then continues to the end of the item, which occurs, say, at point p in the buffer. The item is then converted as necessary (based on the attributes of the current variable needed by the GET statement) and transferred to the location in memory corresponding to that variable. The same process applies to edit-directed input, except that blanks are treated as any other characters.

If there are more data to be transmitted, i.e., the input list is not yet satisfied, the scan then resumes from point p, and subsequent items are converted and transferred to their appropriate locations in memory. The process continues until one of two things happen:

The scan reaches the end of the buffer. In this case, the buffer is re-filled from the file and the scan starts over from the first location in the buffer.

The input list is satisfied. In this case, the operating system saves the location of point p and returns control to the PL/I program. When a subsequent GET statement refers to the same file, the scan will resume from that point.

For output, the process is reversed. The data in each of the items in the output list is converted and placed into the buffer associated with the output file. When the buffer is full, its contents are written on the associated external device and the process begins again. If the output list is exhausted before the buffer is full, the location in the buffer into which the next data item is to be placed is saved; the first data item from the subsequent PUT statement will be placed into the buffer starting at that point. When an output file is closed, either implicitly by the end of the program, or explicitly by a CLOSE statement, an end-of-file character is added to the associated buffer and the contents of the buffer are written into the file. The buffer is then "detached", meaning that that area of memory can be used for some other purpose.

Buffer contents are written on external devices as "physical records." To understand the meaning of this term, suppose we want to write the contents of a buffer on magnetic tape. In order to record the data so that it can later be read, the tape must be brought up to a defined constant speed. After the data are written, the tape must come to a stop, but it cannot stop instantly. The result is that there will be some blank tape on each end of the data record that was written. There are thus distinct "data" and "non-data" areas on the tape. The "data areas" are physical records, and the "non-data" areas are called inter-record gaps. (See the illustration on following page.) We can think of a physical record as being equivalent to one "bufferful" of information.

Once the tape has come up to the proper speed we can write as large a physical record as we like by having a buffer as large as we like. The input buffer required for reading a record back in must be at least as large as the buffer used for writing it because a physical record must be read in all at once just as it must be written out all at once. There is no problem if the input buffer is larger than the physical record to be read; the buffer will merely be incompletely filled.

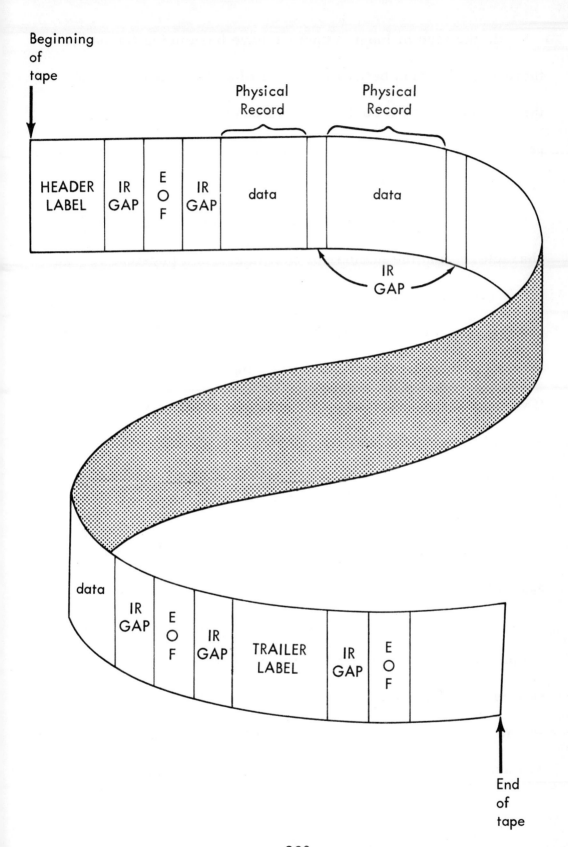

In the kind of input/output we have been using (stream), there is no relation between the size of a physical record and the amount of data it contains. For example, it is perfectly permissible for a data item to be partly contained in one physical record, and partly in the next one.

The contents of physical records in stream files are characters, and the number of characters in a physical record is the same as the number of characters allocated for the buffer, and this number is entirely independent of the number of characters that may be transmitted by an input or output statement. If we want a file to be organized as a stream file, we can say so explicitly in a DECLARE statement:

DECLARE name STREAM ;

We could also specify INPUT or OUTPUT (or PRINT) if appropriate.

Why isn't the FILE attribute used in the above statement? Simply because it isn't needed; the attribute STREAM is sufficient to specify that name is a file. In fact, if we specify any attributes which are applicable only to files, the compiler will assume that the associated name is a file name.

Because the contents of stream files are always characters, i.e., the external form of data, data must be converted during input into the computer's internal form before being stored. During output, data must be converted into characters before being written.

It is frequently useful to organize files so that each physical record contains a certain amount of data, and it happens that in such cases it is unnecessary or undesirable to convert data from internal form to external form. For instance, we might want to write the contents of a structure into a file to be read later. Since the data will be read only by the program, it is wasteful of time to convert the items to external form when writing and then to convert them back into internal form when subsequently reading. Furthermore, if we write the contents of the structure as one physical record, we need a buffer that is just large enough to contain the structure contents. And, since it is unnecessary to convert the contents, why not use the structure itself as the buffer?

The kind of file needed to perform the desired operation is called a RECORD file. The main difference between RECORD and STREAM files is that information in RECORD files is maintained in the computer's internal form on the external device, while information in STREAM files consists of characters. (One consequence of this difference is that PRINT cannot be used as an attribute of a RECORD file.) Because no conversion is performed during record input/output, large quantities of data can be read and written in a relatively short time. From a practical standpoint, this is the major advantage of record input/output.

The input/output statements for RECORD files are READ and WRITE, corresponding to GET and PUT which are used with STREAM files. The general forms of READ and WRITE statements are:

> READ FILE(name) INTO (variable) ;

and

> WRITE FILE(name) FROM (variable) ;

where variable is

a simple variable,

an array name (without subscripts), or

a structure name associated with a major structure

Only one variable may be read or written by a single READ or WRITE statement. However, the name that is used might cause a great deal of data to be transmitted, e.g., it could be the name of a major structure. There is in fact a great advantage in organizing data so that a great deal can be transmitted by a single READ or WRITE statement. Each record input/output statement causes a single record to be transmitted. If the associated file happens to be magnetic tape, for example, and the transmitted records are very short, a very small portion of the tape would be used for data; most of the tape would be inter-record gaps. Thus, we might find it useful to organize a number of simple variables into a structure simply to improve the efficiency of input/output operations. The following two examples show how this might be done:

```
SLOW: PROCEDURE OPTIONS (MAIN) ;

      /* EXAMPLE NO. 45
         INEFFICIENT I/O. */

      DECLARE  FF  RECORD OUTPUT,
               A   FIXED,
               B   FLOAT,
               C CHARACTER(10) ;

      WRITE FILE( FF ) FROM( A ) ;
      WRITE FILE( FF ) FROM( B ) ;
      WRITE FILE( FF ) FROM( C ) ;

      END SLOW ;
```

```
FAST: PROCEDURE OPTIONS (MAIN) ;

        /* EXAMPLE NO. 46
           EFFICIENT I/O. */

        DECLARE  FF  RECORD OUTPUT,

               1 COLLECT,
               2 A   FIXED,
               2 B   FLOAT,
               2 C   CHARACTER(10) ;

        WRITE FILE( FF ) FROM( COLLECT ) ;

     END FAST ;
```

A bank might wish to read data for each of its customers and build a file containing data on those customers whose balances are less than $500. The bank's program might be:

```
LOW_BAL: PROCEDURE OPTIONS (MAIN) ;

        /* EXAMPLE NO. 47
           ESTABLISH FILE OF CUSTOMERS WITH BALANCES
           BELOW $500. */

        DECLARE  CUST_IN  RECORD INPUT,
                 LT500    RECORD OUTPUT,

               1 PROFILE,
               2 NAME,
               3 LAST        CHARACTER(15),
               3 FIRST       CHARACTER(10),
               2 ACCOUNT_NO  FIXED,
               2 BALANCE     FLOAT ;

        ON ENDFILE( CUST_IN ) GO TO OUT ;

NEXT:   READ FILE( CUST_IN ) INTO( PROFILE ) ;

        IF BALANCE<500 THEN
LOW:        WRITE FILE( LT500 ) FROM( PROFILE ) ;
        GO TO NEXT ;

OUT:    CLOSE FILE( LT500 ) ;
        END LOW_BAL ;
```

The data for every customer is checked, and those with balances below $500 are recorded in file LT500, which is organized exactly like CUST_IN, except that there are fewer (presumably) records in LT500. There is very little calculation performed in Example No. 47, but a great deal of input/output is performed. Thus, it is extremely valuable not to have to convert the data during each input/output operation.

Suppose the bank wanted to print the data for each customer whose balance was below $500. That could be done very simply, by replacing the statement at LOW with a PUT statement, possibly a very simple PUT statement referencing the standard output file. If some other file were to be used, it must have been declared with the attributes STREAM and PRINT. Still, only a fraction of the total data to be processed will be converted, since the statement at LOW is not executed for every customer.

The rate of data transmission between an external device and a buffer is very slow compared to the internal speed of the computer, because external devices are mechanical in nature. For this reason, it is sometimes very desirable to, 1) transfer data to a device less frequently, by transferring more of it each time, and 2) avoid having to wait for a buffer to be filled or emptied.

If, in Example No. 47, the buffer had been large enough to hold five replications of the structure PROFILE, the data would have to go to external devices only one-fifth as often as when the buffer is large enough to hold only one copy of PROFILE. Such a buffer could be used, and, in fact might have been set up by the operating system automatically. If such a buffer exists, then each physical record contains a number of replications of PROFILE. Each replication is called a logical record.

In general, the number of logical records in a physical record is called the blocking factor. Usually, the blocking factor will be an integer, greater than or equal to 1, but this is the case only because logical records in a physical record are usually of the same length. There is no requirement that this be the case; we could combine a very short structure and a very long structure together in one physical record. Also, a structure might be longer than the maximum length of a physical record permitted by the operating system; in this case there will be less than one logical record in a physical record. The most important thing to remember about logical records is that they are not distinguishable from one another in the same way that physical records are (except when the blocking factor is 1: in that case, each logical record corresponds to a physical record, and records are distinguishable by inter-record gaps).

Packing several records together in a physical record is one way to minimize the time required to move data between the computer and an external device. Another way is to add more buffers. Suppose, for example we want to write a great deal of data. If only one buffer were available our computation would be suspended by the operating system each time the buffer became full, and would resume only after the contents had been transferred to the external device. If two buffers were available, however, as soon as one became full its contents could be transferred to the external device while our computation could proceed, placing information into the other buffer. Even if the second buffer became full before the first one had been completely emptied, our computation would be suspended for a shorter period of time. A similar situation holds for reading: once we have exhausted one buffer, the system can start filling it again, but in the meantime, our program could start to extract information from the second buffer.

We specify that more than one buffer is to be associated with a file by means of the BUFFERED attribute in the file declaration (or OPEN statement). The BUFFERED attribute must always be used with two other attributes, RECORD - which has been discussed - and SEQUENTIAL, which will be discussed shortly. A typical OPEN statement might be:

OPEN FILE(name) RECORD INPUT SEQUENTIAL BUFFERED ;

to open a buffered input file.

When a file has the BUFFERED attribute we can operate on data while it is in the buffer. Up to this point we have brought data into the buffer and then transferred it to some other area, say, a structure in the program, in order to work on it. The transfer takes time, and also means that we have used twice as much of the computer's memory in some cases; i.e., we have had to have a buffer (for which the operating system allocated space) and a structure which we declared. The similar situation existed for output.

The operating system keeps track of logical records in buffers by means of a "pointer" which always indicates the beginning of a logical record. We can overlay a structure on the buffer, starting at the current pointer position. (When this is done, the structure is said to be <u>based</u> on the pointer.) We can then use the structure in whatever way we wish, but we are really operating on the contents of the buffer. In a sense, we are using the structure to format the data in the buffer.

For an example, we will modify Example No. 47 so that it works on the data in PROFILE not by moving the data in the buffer to the structure, but by moving the structure to the data in the buffer.

```
LOW_BAL: PROCEDURE OPTIONS (MAIN) ;

            /* EXAMPLE NO. 48
               ESTABLISH FILE OF CUSTOMERS WITH BALANCES
               BELOW $500. DO NOT MOVE DATA FROM BUFFERS,
               BUT TRANSFER DATA DIRECTLY FROM INPUT TO
               OUTPUT BUFFER WHEN NECESSARY TO WRITE. */

            DECLARE  CUST_IN   SEQUENTIAL RECORD BUFFERED INPUT,
                     LT500     SEQUENTIAL RECORD OUTPUT BUFFERED,

                     1 PROFILE   CONTROLLED( BASE ),
                      2 NAME,
                       3 LAST         CHARACTER(15),
                       3 FIRST        CHARACTER(10),
                      2 ACCOUNT_NO  FIXED,
                      2 BALANCE     FLOAT ;

            ON ENDFILE( CUST_IN ) GO TO OUT ;

   NEXT:    READ FILE( CUST_IN ) SET( BASE ) ;

            IF BALANCE<500 THEN
   LOW:         LOCATE PROFILE SET( BASE ) FILE( LT500 ) ;

            GO TO NEXT ;

   OUT:     CLOSE FILE( LT500 ) ;

            END LOW_BAL ;
```

It is very important to recognize that none of the computer memory is set aside for the structure PROFILE in Example No. 48, as it was in Example No. 47. Rather, the structure declaration in Example No. 48 serves merely to define a pattern which can be overlaid on data in a buffer. The variable BASE is a arbitrary identifier, which, because of the context in Example No. 48 is called a <u>pointer variable</u>. The same variable is used in the READ statement at NEXT, and the effect is to overlay the pattern associated with BASE, i.e., PROFILE, on the data in the buffer. Then, when we refer to BALANCE in the next statement, we are really referring to the data in the buffer that lies under that part of the pattern.

It is useful to compare the kind of READ statement used here with the kind of READ statement we have used before.

READ FILE(<u>name</u>) INTO(<u>variable</u>) ;

causes data to be read from the file named <u>name</u> into a buffer, and thence to the computer memory location corresponding to variable. Variable may

be a simple variable, an array without subscripts,

or a major structure.

READ FILE(name) SET(pointer) ;

causes data to be read from the file named name

into a buffer, and then the pattern controlled by

pointer is associated with the record. The

pattern name (which does not appear explicitly

in the READ statement) is called a based

variable. The file name must have the attri-

butes BUFFERED, RECORD, SEQUENTIAL,

and INPUT. These attributes may be specified

in any sequence.* Note: The pattern must not

contain any elements having the VARYING

attribute.

---

* Further, some may be specified in the file declaration, and
the rest in an OPEN statement. If the file is opened implicitly,
then all must appear in the declaration.

The LOCATE statement at LOW in Example No. 48 is used to place data directly into an output buffer. The data are transferred from the input buffer (more precisely, from that part of the input buffer that lies under the pattern PROFILE) into the buffer associated with the file LT500. The general form of the LOCATE statement is:

LOCATE pattern SET(pointer) FILE(name) ;

where pattern is a based variable and pointer is the pointer variable associated with it. Pattern must be the name of a major structure.

A LOCATE statement causes data to be placed in a buffer, where it remains until another LOCATE or a WRITE statement is executed. At that time, the buffer may be emptied to an external device, or the buffer pointer may be repositioned to point to the next logical record to be placed in the buffer.

The file name associated with a LOCATE statement must have the attributes BUFFERED, RECORD, SEQUENTIAL, and OUTPUT. These attributes may be specified in any sequence.

What is a sequential file? As the name implies, a sequential file is one in which the records are organized sequentially; to access a particular record it is necessary to go through the file, beginning with the first record, until the particular record is found. All files can be sequential.

A direct access file, in contrast to a sequential file, is one from which records can be extracted (or written) in any sequence. The concept of the "next record" does not apply to direct access files. Consequently, among other things, direct access files cannot have the BUFFERED attribute.

Whether an external device can be associated with a direct access file depends on its physical characteristics. Card readers, printers, and magnetic tape units cannot be associated with direct access files; they are sequential devices. Other devices, such as magnetic disk units, can be associated with direct access or sequential files.

In order to access a particular record in a direct access file, we must have some way of identifying the record. Records are identified by "keys" which determine their positions in the file. Every direct access file operation must reference a key, and the length of the key must be specified, perhaps outside the PL/I program.

A direct access file is declared by a statement of the form:

DECLARE <u>name</u> RECORD DIRECT KEYED

where all of the indicated attributes must appear, but not
necessarily in that order. The INPUT or OUTPUT attribute
may also be specified.

A typical use of a direct access file might be to maintain
personnel records as part of a management information system.
To access the record pertaining to a particular employee, we
do not want to search through all of the records until we find
the one we want.

Each record must have a unique key. Assuming that the
key for a given record is the associated employee's social
security number, we can write a program which will accept
social security numbers and print the appropriate employees'
personnel records.

```
EMPL2:    PROCEDURE OPTIONS (MAIN) ;

          /* EXAMPLE NO. 49
          READ SOCIAL SECURITY NUMBERS AND PRINT
          EMPLOYEE RECORD ACCESSED FROM DIRECT
          ACCESS FILE.
          NOTE:
          THE DECLARE STATEMENT FOR 'FILENAME' IS
          NOT ADEQUATE FOR ALL IMPLEMENTATIONS OF
          PL/I.   ADDITIONAL INFORMATION MAY BE
          REQUIRED BY THE OPERATING SYSTEM.   */
```

```
          DECLARE  1 EMPLOYEE,
                    2 NAME,
                     3 LAST        CHARACTER(15),
                     3 FIRST       CHARACTER(10),
                    2 SOCIAL_SECURITY  FIXED DECIMAL(9),
                     /* USED AS RECORD KEY */
                    2 DEPARTMENT  FIXED DECIMAL(3),
                    2 RATE_OF_PAY,
                     3 REGULAR     FLOAT,
                     3 OVERTIME    FLOAT,
                    2 DATE_OF_LAST_REVIEW CHARACTER(6) ;

          DECLARE  EMPLFIL  RECORD DIRECT KEYED INPUT ;

NEXT:     GET LIST( SOCIAL_SECURITY ) ;

          /* ACCESS EMPLOYEE'S RECORD FROM DIRECT ACCESS
             FILE. */
          READ FILE( EMPLFIL ) INTO( EMPLOYEE )
                                KEY( SOCIAL_SECURITY ) ;

          /* PRINT RECORD */
          PUT LIST( EMPLOYEE ) SKIP ;

          GO TO NEXT ;

      END EMPL2 ;
```

The key specified in the READ statement in Example No.
49 is used by the computer to find the desired record, but we
need not concern ourselves with how a social security number
is transformed into a record location on a direct access device.

The general form of the READ statement referencing a
direct access file is:

READ FILE(<u>name</u>) INTO(<u>variable</u>) KEY(<u>expression</u>) ;

The WRITE statement for a direct access file is similar,
except that KEY becomes KEYFROM:

WRITE FILE(<u>name</u>) FROM(<u>variable</u>) KEYFROM(<u>expression</u>) ;

In the case of WRITE, the KEYFROM expression is converted to a character string. This string is the key for the record to be written. It is placed into the buffer ahead of the information in <u>variable</u>. The KEYFROM expression also determines the position of the record in the file.

In the case of READ, the KEY expression is converted to a character string which determines the position of the record in the file. This record is then read into <u>variable</u>.

Now we can write a PL/I program that could be used to create the file that is accessed by Example No. 49.

```
EMPL1:   PROCEDURE OPTIONS (MAIN) ;

            /* EXAMPLE NO. 50
               CREATE DIRECT ACCESS FILE FOR USE BY
               EXAMPLE NO. 49
               NOTE:
               THE DECLARE STATEMENT FOR 'FILENAME' IS
               NOT ADEQUATE FOR ALL IMPLEMENTATIONS OF
               PL/I.  ADDITIONAL INFORMATION MAY BE
               REQUIRED BY THE OPERATING SYSTEM.  */

            DECLARE  1 EMPLOYEE,
                       2 NAME,
                        3 LAST        CHARACTER(15),
                        3 FIRST       CHARACTER(10),
                       2 SOCIAL_SECURITY FIXED DECIMAL(9),
                        /* USED AS RECORD KEY */
                       2 DEPARTMENT   FIXED DECIMAL(3),
                       2 RATE_OF_PAY,
                        3 REGULAR     FLOAT,
                        3 OVERTIME    FLOAT,
                       2 DATE_OF_LAST_REVIEW CHARACTER(6) ;

            DECLARE  EMPLFIL  RECORD DIRECT KEYED OUTPUT ;
```

```
NEXT:      /* READ EMPLOYEE'S RECORD FROM STANDARD INPUT
             FILE. */
          GET LIST( EMPLOYEE ) ;

          /* PLACE RECORD IN DIRECT ACCESS FILE. */
          WRITE FILE( EMPLFIL ) FROM( EMPLOYEE )
                              KEYFROM( SOCIAL_SECURITY ) ;

          GO TO NEXT ;

       END EMPL1 ;
```

Direct access files are most advantageous when there are

many records in a file, but it is necessary to process only a few

of them. They are also superior to sequential files (in terms of

time required) when it is necessary to process records in random

order.

Sequential files, on the other hand, are more useful when

a large proportion of the records in a file are to be processed,

since it usually takes less time to access the "next" record in a

sequential file than it does to access a random record in a direct

access file.

The records in a direct access file can be organized

sequentially, i.e., records can be placed in the file in ascend-

ing order, by key; an organization of this kind combines the best

features of both organizations. For example, this is the best

organization for processing a number of sequential records, the

first of which is somewhere near the middle of the file. A

typical example is a company which sends out invoices at certain times of the month to all customers whose names begin with a certain letter; the customers' records are placed in the file alphabetically, so the first customer whose name begins with a certain letter can be found quickly through direct access. The rest of the names would appear in sequence in subsequent records.

APPENDIX A

CHARACTER SETS AND OPERATORS

I.   60-CHARACTER SET

Graphic	Description
A thru Z	Alphabetic
$, @ , #	Alphabetic
0 thru 9	Numeric
	Blank
=	Equal or replacement
+	Plus
-	Minus
*	Asterisk
/	Slash
(	Left parenthesis
)	Right parenthesis
,	Comma

.	Radix point or qualification
'	Quote
%	Percent
;	Semicolon
:	Colon
__	Break character
¬	Not
&	And
|	Or
<	Less Than
>	Greater Than
?	Question mark

II. 48-CHARACTER SET

Graphic	Description
A thru Z	Alphabetic
$	Alphabetic
0 thru 9	Numeric
	Blank
=	Equal or replacement

+	Plus
-	Minus
*	Asterisk
/	Slash
(	Left parenthesis
)	Right parenthesis
,	Comma
.	Radix point or qualification
'	Quote

Some language elements require two graphics for their representation in the 48-character set. These are:

Element	48-Character Representation
Semicolon	, .
Colon	. .
Percent	/ /

No blanks may appear between the two graphics constituting a single element. To avoid confusion, at least one blank should appear to either side of a two-graphic element.

III. OPERATORS

	Operator	
Operation	60-Char.	48-Char.*
Assignment	=	=
Exponentiation	**	**
Multiplication	*	*
Division	/	/
Addition	+	+
Subtraction	-	-
Negation (arithmetic)	-	-
Negation (logical)	¬	NOT
And	&	AND
Or	|	OR
Less than	<	LT
Less than or equal	< =	LE
Equal	=	=
Greater than or equal	> =	GE
Greater than	>	GT
Not equal	¬ =	NE
Not less than	¬ <	NL
Not greater than	¬ >	NG
Concatenation	||	CAT
Qualification	.	.
Begin comment	/*	/*
End comment	*/	*/

---

*   Operators composed of alphabetic characters must be delimited by one or more blanks on both sides. Alphabetic operators may not be used as identifiers; they are "reserved" words.

APPENDIX B

KEYWORD ABBREVIATIONS

BINARY	BIN
CHARACTER	CHAR
CONVERSION	CONV
DECIMAL	DEC
DECLARE	DCL
EXTERNAL	EXT
FIXEDOVERFLOW	FOFL
INITIAL	INIT
OVERFLOW	OFL
PICTURE	PIC
PROCEDURE	PROC
SUBSCRIPTRANGE	SUBRG
UNDERFLOW	UFL
VARYING	VAR
ZERODIVIDE	ZDIV

APPENDIX C

BUILT-IN FUNCTIONS

I.   ARITHMETIC

Function values have the same base, scale, and precision as the arguments. Arguments to trigonometric functions are assumed to be expressed in radians.

Function	Value
ABS(arg)	The absolute value of arg.
ATAN(arg)	ABS(arctan(arg)) modulo $\pi/2$.
ATAN(arg1, arg2)	arctan (arg1/arg2). The result is positioned in the correct quadrant. Error if arg1 = 0 and arg2 = 0.

CEIL(arg)	The smallest integer greater than or equal to arg.
	Example: X = -1.23;
	          Y = CEIL(X) ;
	          then Y contains -1.

COMPLEX(arg1, arg2)	Arg1 becomes the real part and arg2 becomes the imaginary part of the complex function value.
CONJ(arg)	The complex conjugate of arg.

Function	Value
COS($\underline{arg}$)	cos($\underline{arg}$)
COSH($\underline{arg}$)	cosh($\underline{arg}$)
EXP($\underline{arg}$)	$e^{\underline{arg}}$
FLOOR($\underline{arg}$)	The largest integer less than or equal to $\underline{arg}$. Example: X = 1.23; Y = FLOOR(X) ; then Y contains 1.
IMAG($\underline{arg}$)	The imaginary part of $\underline{arg}$.
LOG($\underline{arg}$)	ln($\underline{arg}$). Error if $\underline{arg} \leq 0$.
LOG2($\underline{arg}$)	$\log_2(\underline{arg})$. Error if $\underline{arg} < 0$.
LOG10($\underline{arg}$)	$\log_{10}(\underline{arg})$. Error if $\underline{arg} \leq 0$.
MAX($\underline{arg1}$, $\underline{arg2}$,...)	The maximum value of an arbitrary number of arguments. Example: A = 1; B = 2; C = 3; D = -2; Z = MAX(A,B,C,D) ; then Z contains 3
MIN($\underline{arg1}$, $\underline{arg2}$,...)	The minimum value of an arbitrary number of arguments. Example: A = 1; B = 2; C = 3; D = -2; Z = MIN(A,B,C,D) ; then Z contains -2.

319

Function	Value
MOD(arg1, arg2)	The remainder of (arg1/arg2). Example: A = 16; B = 3; Z = MOD(A,B) ; then Z contains 1.
REAL(arg)	The real part of arg.
SIGN(arg)	1 if arg > 0 0 if arg = 0 -1 if arg < 0
SIN(arg)	sin(arg)
SINH(arg)	sinh(arg)
SQRT(arg)	Positive square root of arg. Error if arg < 0.
TAN(arg)	tan(arg)
TANH(arg)	tanh(arg)
TRUNC(arg)	The arg truncated to an integer. Examples: A = 1.875; B = -3.625; Y = TRUNC(A) ; Y contains 1. Z = TRUNC(B) ; Z contains -3.

II. STRING FUNCTIONS

Function	Value
INDEX(arg1, arg2)	The position in the string arg1 where arg2 first appears as a substring. If arg2 does not occur the value returned is zero. Example:

```
DECLARE A CHARACTER(8), Z FIXED ;
A = 'COMPUTER';
Z  =  INDEX (A, 'MP') ;
Z contains 3.
X  =  INDEX (A, 'Y') ;
X contains 0.
```

Function	Value
LENGTH(arg)	The length of the string, arg.
SUBSTR(arg1, s, n)	A substring of the string, arg1. The substring starts at position s of arg1 and is n characters long. If n is omitted then the substring starts at position s in arg1 and continues to the end of arg1. Example:

```
DECLARE (A,Z) CHARACTER(8) VARYING ;
A = 'COMPUTER' ;
Z  =  SUBSTR(A, 4, 3) ;
Z contains the character string PUT.
```

Function	Value
UNSPEC(arg)	The bit string which is the internal representation of arg.

III.   ARRAY FUNCTIONS

The arguments noted as <u>arg</u> to the following functions must be unsubscripted array names. The arguments noted as <u>n</u> must be integer expressions.

Function	Value
ALL(<u>arg</u>)	A bit string equal in length to the length of the greatest element of <u>arg</u>. If there is a 1 in the same bit position of every element, the corresponding bit position in the result contains 1. Otherwise, the corresponding bit position in the result contains 0.

Example: A(1) = 5 ; A(2) = 3 ;
Y = ALL(A) ;
A(1) contains 101
A(2) contains 011
Y contains 001

ANY(<u>arg</u>)	A bit string equal in length to the length of the greatest element of <u>arg</u>. If there is a 1 in any bit position of any element, the corresponding bit position in the result contains 1. Otherwise, the corresponding bit position in the result contains 0.

Example: A(1) = 5 ; A(2) = 3 ;
Y = ANY(A)
A(1) contains 101
A(2) contains 011
Y contains 111

Function	Value

DIM(<u>arg</u>, <u>n</u>)	The extent of the <u>n</u>th dimension of <u>arg</u>.
	Example: DCL A(5, 10, 20) ;
	            Y = DIM(A,2) ;
	            Y contains 10.

HBOUND(<u>arg</u>, <u>n</u>)	The upper bound of the <u>n</u>th dimension of <u>arg</u>.

LBOUND(<u>arg</u>, <u>n</u>)	The lower bound of the <u>n</u>th dimension of <u>arg</u>.
	Example: DECLARE A(-1:10) ;
	            DO I=LBOUND(A,1)
	               to HBOUND(A,1) ;
	            means
	            DO I=-1 to 10 ;

PROD(<u>arg</u>)	The product of all the elements of <u>arg</u>.
	Example: DECLARE A(3) ;
	            A(1)=1; A(2)=5; A(3)=10;
	            Y = PROD(A) ;
	            Y contains 50.

SUM(<u>arg</u>)	The sum of all the elements of <u>arg</u>.
	Example: DECLARE A(3) ;
	            A(1)=1; A(2)=5; A(3)=10;
	            Y = SUM(A) ;
	            Y contains 16.

IV.   MISCELLANEOUS FUNCTIONS

Function	Value
DATE	Character string of form YYMMDD: YY=Year MM=Month DD=Day
ROUND(arg, p)	arg rounded to the pth digit after the decimal point.
TIME	Character string of form HHMMSSTTT: HH=Hours MM=Minutes SS=Seconds TTT=Milliseconds

APPENDIX D

CONDITIONS

The classification of conditions into "initially enabled" and "initially disabled" classes holds for the IBM System/360 computer. Some conditions may fall into the other class when other computers are used.

A more complete and detailed list of conditions is given in PL/I Language Specifications, IBM Form C28-6571.

I. INITIALLY ENABLED CONDITIONS

The following conditions are enabled initially; some of them may be disabled by means of prefixes (see Chapter 9).

Condition	Description
CONDITION(name)	Raised by a SIGNAL statement. Name is a programmer defined condition. Standard action: comment and continue.

Condition	Description
CONVERSION	Raised when a character conversion is illegal or arithmetic value exceeds the width of the field. Raised internally or during I/O. Result is undefined. Standard action: raise the ERROR condition.
ENDFILE(filename)	Raised during a GET or READ statement when an attempt is made to read past an end of file. Standard action: raise the ERROR condition.
ENDPAGE(filename)	Raised when an attempt is made to write on the line beyond the maximum for the page. Standard action: start new page.
ERROR	Raised by a SIGNAL statement, or as standard action for other conditions. Standard action: terminate the program.
FIXEDOVERFLOW	Raised when a fixed point number exceeds the field width allowed for it. Result is undefined. Standard action: comment and continue.
KEY(filename)	Raised when a key is not found when reading a keyed record. Raised when trying to WRITE or LOCATE a key that already exists. Standard action: raise the ERROR condition.
NAME(filename)	Raised during a data-directed GET statement if an unrecognizable identifier is found. Standard action: comment and continue.

Condition	Description
OVERFLOW	Raised when the exponent of a floating point number exceeds maximum. Result is undefined. Standard action: raise the ERROR condition.
UNDERFLOW	Raised when an exponent of a floating point number is smaller than permitted minimum. Result is zero. Standard action: comment and continue.
ZERODIVIDE	Raised when an attempt is made to divide by zero. Result is undefined. Standard action: raise the ERROR condition.

II. INITIALLY DISABLED CONDITIONS

The following conditions must be enabled by prefixes (see Chapter 9) before they will be raised.

Condition	Description
CHECK(list)	Raised when the value of a variable named in the list is changed, when a statement named in the list is executed, and when a procedure named in the list is called. Standard system action: comment and continue.
SIZE	Raised during a conversion between different scales or bases or precision if high-order bits will be lost. Result is undefined. Standard action: raise the ERROR condition.

Condition	Description
SUBSCRIPTRANGE	Raised when a subscript is outside the declared bounds. Result is undefined. Standard action: raise the ERROR condition.

APPENDIX E

PICTURE AND FORMAT SPECIFICATIONS

I.   PICTURE CHARACTERS

Character	Meaning
9	The associated position contains a decimal digit. Example: If A=51 and is printed with a picture of '999' it will appear as 051
V	The associated position contains decimal point scaling. It does not specify the point. Example: If A=51.1 and is edited with a picture of '999V9' it will appear as 0511
K	The associated position indicates the beginning of the exponent. Example: If A=53.1 and is edited with a picture of '999K99' it will appear as 53102
E	The associated position will contain the letter E indicating the beginning of the exponent. Example: If A=53.1 and is edited with a picture of '999E99' it will appear as 531E02

Character	Meaning

.

The associated position will contain the character .
Example: If A=53.1 and is edited with a picture of '999V.9' it will appear as 053.1

Z

The associated position will be made blank if it contains a leading zero. Otherwise, it contains the digit.
Example: If A=53.1 and is edited with a picture of 'Z99V.99' it will appear as 53.1

B

The associated position will contain a blank.
Example: If A=53.1 and is edited with a picture of 'B999V.99' it will appear as 053.1

Y

The associated position will be made blank if it contains a zero, leading or otherwise.

-

The associated field will contain a minus sign if the number is negative and will be made blank otherwise.
If there are two or more consecutive minus signs, the minus sign will drift.
Example: If A=-53.1 and is edited with a picture of '-9999V9' it will appear as -00531
If the picture is '----9V9' it will appear as -531

Character	Meaning
+	The associated field will contain a plus sign if the number is positive and will be made blank otherwise. If there are two or more consecutive plus signs, the plus sign will drift. Example: If A=53.1 and is edited with a picture of '+9999V99' it will appear as +005310 If the picture is '+++99V9' it will appear as +531
S	The associated field will contain a plus sign or minus sign depending on the value of the number. If there are two or more consecutive "S" the sign will drift. Example: If A=-5.2 and B=71 and they are edited with a picture of 'S999V.99' they will appear as -005.20 and +071.00 If they are edited with a picture of 'SS99V.9' they will appear as -05.2 and +71.0
$	The associated position will contain a $. If there are two or more consecutive "$" the sign will drift. Example: If A=106.75 and is edited with a picture of '$9999V.99' it will appear as $0106.75 If it is edited with a picture of '$$$99V.99' it will appear as $106.75

Character	Meaning
,	The associated position will contain a comma. Example: If A=102791 and is edited with a picture of '999,999.' it will appear as <u>102,791</u>.
CR	The associated two positions will contain the letters "CR" if the number is negative and two blanks otherwise. CR must appear to the right of all the digits. Example: If A=-5.35 and is edited with a picture of '$999V.99BCR' it will appear as <u>$005.35 CR</u>
DB	The same as for CR except that DB will appear.
A	The associated position may contain an alphabetic character or a blank. Example: If A='THE COMPUTER' and is edited with a picture of 'AAAAAAAAAAAA' it will appear as <u>THE COMPUTER</u>
X	The associated position may contain any alphabetic character, any digit, or a blank. Example: If A='THE COMPUTER' and B=663 and they are both edited with a picture of 'XXXXXXXXXXX' they will appear as <u>THE COMPUTER</u> and <u>663</u>

II. FORMAT SPECIFICATIONS

Specification		Meaning

A or
A(w)

Input: Treat the next w characters as alphabetic (character string) data. W must be specified.

Output: Treat the corresponding data item as a character string of length w, extending it on the right with blanks or truncating from the right if necessary. If w is not specified it is taken as the current length of the item. Example: If X = 'CAT' and is edited with A or A(3) it will appear as CAT; edited with A(1) it will appear as C; and edited with A(5) it will appear as CATbb.

B or
B(w)

Input: Read a bit string from the next w-character field. The string need not fill the field. W must be specified.

Output: Treat the corresponding data item as a bit string of length w, extending it on the right with blanks or truncating from the right if necessary. If w is not specified it is taken as the current length of the item.

Specification	Meaning

C(spec) or
C(spec, spec)

Read or write a complex numeric data item. Each spec is one of the specifications F, E, or P. If two specifications are used the first applies to the real part of the item; the second to the imaginary part. If only one specification is used it applies to both parts of the item.

E(w, d) or
E(w, d, s)

Input: Read a floating-point number from the next w-character field. The number need not fill the field. The rightmost d digits are assumed to follow the decimal point unless an explicit decimal point appears elsewhere in the field.

Output: Write a floating-point number in the next w-character field. S is the number of significant digits to be written; d is the number of digits to be written following the decimal point. If s is omitted it is taken to be d+1. W must be greater than d+5. If d=0 the decimal point will appear; if d < 0 it will not.
Example: If A=123.45 and is edited with E(10,4) it will appear as 1.2345E+02; edited with E(10,2,4) it will appear as 12.34E+01.

334

Specification	Meaning
F(w) or F(w, d) or F(w, d, p)	**Input:** Read a fixed-point number from the next w-character field. The number need not fill the field. The rightmost d digits are assumed to follow the decimal point unless an explicit decimal point appears elsewhere in the field.
	Output: Write a fixed-point number in the next w-character field. If p is specified the number will be scaled by multiplying by 10^p before writing. If p and/or d are omitted they are assumed to be 0. If d is specified to be 0 the decimal point will appear; if d< 0 or is omitted, the point will not appear. <u>Example:</u> If A=-1.23 and is edited with F(2) it will appear as -1; edited with F(3, 0) it will appear as -1.; edited with F(5, -1, 3) it will appear as -1230.
P'specs'	<u>Specs</u> comprise a string of picture characters as shown in Part I of this appendix.
R(label)	Transfer the editing function to the FORMAT statement at <u>label</u>.
X(w)	**Input:** Ignore the next w characters.
	Output: Insert w blanks into the output stream.

335

1.1   The identifiers are

A_B TIME $_AMOUNT IBM VARIABLE S360 X1Y2

The non-identifiers are

A*B PL/I ACCOUNT-NUMBER (TEMP)

1.2   <u>Expression</u>   <u>PL/I Equivalent</u>

x^3 X**3

$(x - 1) (x + 1)$ (X - 1) * (X + 1)

$x^2 + 2x + 1$ X**2 + 2*X + 1 or, preferably,
                                       X*(X + 2) + 1

$\sqrt{a^2 + b^2}$ SQRT(A**2 + B**2)

$\dfrac{a + b + c}{3}$ (A + B + C)/3

1.3

```
EX1_3:    PROCEDURE OPTIONS (MAIN) ;

          /* SOLUTION TO EXERCISE 1.3 */

          DECLARE ( A, B, C ) FLOAT ;
          GET LIST( A, B ) ;
          C = SQRT( A**2 + B**2 ) ;
          PUT LIST( A, B, C ) ;
        END EX1_3 ;
```

1.4

```
EX1_4:    PROCEDURE OPTIONS (MAIN) ;

          /* SOLUTION TO EXERCISE 1.4 */

          DECLARE ( GROSS, TAX, NET ) FLOAT ;
          GET LIST( GROSS ) ;
          TAX = 0.22*GROSS ;
          NET = GROSS - TAX ;
          PUT LIST( GROSS, TAX, NET ) ;
     END EX1_4 ;
```

1.5   The answers may differ because the fractions used cannot

be exactly represented in the computer. Errors due to

this fact are discussed more fully in Chapter 4.

2.1   The use of the variable DISC makes it unnecessary to
evaluate the expression B**2 - 4*A*C more than once,
with the result that the program will execute faster. Also,
the identifier DISC helps to clarify what the program is
doing in the statements where roots are computed.

2.2   1)   R = 3
              R = 2
              R = 1

      2)   R = 1
              R = 2
              R = 1

2.3

```
EX2_3:     PROCEDURE OPTIONS (MAIN) ; ▪

               /* SOLUTION TO EXERCISE 2.3 */

               DECLARE ( S1, S2, S3,      /* SIDES OF TRIANGLE */
                         TYPE ) FLOAT ; /* RELATION OF SIDES */

START:         TYPE = 0 ;
               GET LIST( S1, S2, S3 ) ;

               /* S1, S2, AND S3 FORM A TRIANGLE IF EACH IS
                  LESS THAN THE SUM OF THE OTHER TWO. IS THIS
                  THE CASE -- */

               IF (S1+S2>S3) & ( S2+S3>S1) & (S1+S3>S2) THEN
                  /* THEY FORM A TRIANGLE */
                  TYPE = 1 ;
```

338

```
            ELSE    /* THIS COULD BE TERMINAL CASE */
                    IF S1+S2+S3=0 THEN GO TO STOP ;
                    ELSE GO TO PRINT ; /* NO TRIANGLE */

            /* IS TRIANGLE ISOSCELES -- */

            IF (S1=S2) | (S1=S3) | (S2=S3) THEN
                /* TRIANGLE IS ISOSCELES */
                TYPE = 2 ;

            /* IS TRIANGLE EQUILATERAL -- */

            IF (S1=S2) & (S1=S3) THEN
                /* TRIANGLE IS EQUILATERAL */
                TYPE = 3 ;

PRINT:      /* PRINT RESULTS */
            PUT LIST( S1, S2, S3, TYPE ) ;

            GO TO START ;
STOP:   END EX2_3 ;
```

2.4

```
EX2_4:  PROCEDURE OPTIONS (MAIN) ;

            /* SOLUTION TO EXERCISE 2.4 */

            DECLARE ( S1, S2, S3,     /* THE THREE SIDES */
                      LONG,           /* LONGEST SIDE */
                      TYPE ) FLOAT ; /* RELATION OF SIDES */

START:      TYPE = 0 ;
            GET LIST( S1, S2, S3 ) ;

            /* DO WE HAVE A TRIANGLE -- */

            IF (S1+S2>S3) & (S2+S3>S1) & (S1+S3>S2) THEN
                /* WE HAVE A TRIANGLE */
                TYPE = 1 ;

            ELSE    /* THIS COULD BE TERMINAL CASE */
                    IF S1+S2+S3=0 THEN GO TO STOP ;
                    ELSE GO TO PRINT ;

            /* IS TRIANGLE ISOSCELES -- */

            IF (S1=S2) | (S1=S3) | (S2=S3) THEN
                /* TRIANGLE IS ISOSCELES */
                TYPE = 2 ;
```

339

```
            /* IS IT A RIGHT TRIANGLE -- */

            /* FIND LONGEST SIDE */
            LONG = S1 ;
            IF S2>LONG THEN LONG = S2 ;
            IF S3>LONG THEN LONG = S3 ;

            /* SEE IF PYTHAGOREAN THEOREM HOLDS */
            IF (S1**2+S2**2+S3**2-LONG**2)=LONG**2 THEN
               /* IT DOES */
               DO ;
                  TYPE = TYPE + 3 ;
                  GO TO PRINT ; /* CAN'T BE EQUILATERAL */
               END ;

            /* IS TRIANGLE EQUILATERAL -- */

            IF (S1=S2) & (S1=S3) THEN
               /* TRIANGLE IS EQUILATERAL */
               TYPE = 3 ;

PRINT:      /* PRINT RESULTS */
            PUT LIST( S1, S2, S3, TYPE ) ;

            GO TO START ;
STOP:    END EX2_4 ;
```

2.5   Yes, A = B = C is a legal PL/I statement. It is an assignment statement; the variable A will receive the value 1 or
0 depending on whether B and C are or are not equal,
respectively. The first = is thus an assignment operator,
and the second = is a relational operator. The difference
in meaning is determined from the context.

3.1 A: -99999 to 99999 in steps of 1

     B: -99999 to 99999 in steps of 0.00001 to 1, depending
              on its value. There will always be five significant
              digits because the decimal point "floats."

     C: -999.99 to 999.99 in steps of 0.01

     D: -7 to 7 in steps of 1. The largest magnitude
              expressible in three binary digits is 111, or
              7 decimal.

3.2 <u>Constant</u>   <u>Attributes</u>   <u>Notes</u>

     123   FIXED DECIMAL(3,0)

     'CAT'   CHARACTER(3)

     '''CAUSE'   CHARACTER(6)   The first character is a
                                             quote mark; the second
                                             through sixth are the
                                             letters.

     -3.75   FIXED DECIMAL(3,2)   Neither the minus sign
                                             nor the decimal point
                                             counts as a digit.

     0.03   FIXED DECIMAL(3,2)   The leading zero is signi-
                                             ficant to the precision of
                                             the number.

     .03   FIXED DECIMAL(2,2)

3.3 As a general rule, it is a good idea to organize IF statements so that the conditions most likely to be true are tested first. Testing a condition takes time; if the condition is not true, the time is wasted.

3.4 1, -2, 3, -4, 5, -6, 7, -8, 9, -10

4.1   The number of elements in an array is the product of the

number of elements in each dimension. Hence, the array

NAME(9, 0:9, 0:9, 0:9) has 9x10x10x10 = 9000 elements.

4.2   The sum of the elements in array A, i.e., SUM1 will be

high by a factor of ten since each element of A is added

into the sum ten times instead of just once. The correct

answer can thus be obtained by dividing the printed answer

by ten.

4.3

```
EX4_3:    PROCEDURE OPTIONS (MAIN) ;

               /* SOLUTION TO EXERCISE 4.3 -
                  FIND LARGEST VALUE IN ARRAY */

               DECLARE   ( A(20), LARGE ) FIXED DECIMAL (5,2),
                           I   FIXED BINARY ;

START:         /* READ THE NUMBERS */
               GET LIST( A ) ;

               /* INITIALIZE 'LARGE' */
               LARGE = A(1) ;

               /* FIND LARGEST NUMBER */
               DO I = 2 BY 1 TO 20 ;
                   IF A(I)>LARGE THEN LARGE = A(I) ;
               END ;

               /* PRINT RESULTS */
               PUT LIST( A, LARGE ) ;

               GO TO START;
           END EX4_3 ;
```

4.4

```
EX4_4:    PROCEDURE OPTIONS (MAIN) ;

          /* SOLUTION TO EXERCISE 4.4
             MATRIX MULTIPLICATION */

          DECLARE  ( A, B, C )(15,15) FLOAT,
                   ( I, J, K )            FIXED BINARY,
                   SUM  FLOAT ;

          /* READ VALUES FOR MATRICES 'A' AND 'B' */
          GET LIST( A, B ) ;

          /* FORM PRODUCT IN 'C' */

          DO I = 1 BY 1 TO 15 ;

             DO J = 1 BY 1 TO 15 ;

                SUM = 0 ;

                DO K = 1 BY 1 TO 15 ;

                   SUM = SUM + A(I,K)*B(K,J) ;

                END ;

                C(I,J) = SUM ;

             END ;
          END ;

          /* PRINT RESULTS */
          PUT LIST( A, B, C ) ;
       END EX4_4 ;
```

4.5

```
EX4_5:    PROCEDURE OPTIONS (MAIN) ;

          /* SOLUTION TO EXERCISE 4.5 */

          DECLARE  LETTERS(15)      CHARACTER(1),
                   ( POSITION(0:15), I ) FIXED ;

START:    /* INITIALIZATION */
          POSITION = 0 ;
          /* READ CHARACTERS INTO 'LETTERS' */
          GET LIST( LETTERS ) ;
```

344

```
          /* SCAN FOR 'Q' */

          DO I = 1 BY 1 TO 15 ;
             IF LETTERS(I)='Q' THEN
                DO ;
                   /* UPDATE COUNT OF 'Q'S */
                   POSITION(0) = POSITION(0) + 1 ;

                   /* ADD LATEST POSITION OF OCCURRENCE
                      TO NEXT ELEMENT OF LIST */
                   POSITION( POSITION(0) ) = I ;
                END ;
          END ;

          /* PRINT RESULTS */
          PUT LIST( LETTERS, POSITION ) ;

          GO TO START ;
       END EX4_5 ;
```

4.6

```
   EX4_6:     PROCEDURE OPTIONS (MAIN) ;

                 /* SOLUTION TO EXERCISE 4.6 */

                 DECLARE ( LETTERS(15), KEY ) CHARACTER(1),
                         ( POSITION(0:15), I ) FIXED ;

                 /* INITIALIZATION */
   START:        POSITION = 0 ;
                 GET LIST( KEY ) ;

                 /* READ CHARACTERS INTO 'LETTERS' */
                 GET LIST( LETTERS ) ;

                 /* SCAN FOR KEY */

                 DO I = 1 BY 1 TO 15 ;
                    IF LETTERS(I)=KEY THEN
                       DO ;
                          /* UPDATE COUNT OF APPEARANCES
                             OF KEY CHARACTER */
                          POSITION(0) = POSITION(0) + 1 ;

                          /* RECORD THE POSITION OF ITS LATEST
                             APPEARANCE IN THE NEXT VACANT
                             ELEMENT OF 'POSITION' */
                          POSITION( POSITION(0) ) = I ;
                       END ;
                 END ;

                 /* PRINT RESULTS */
                 PUT LIST( KEY, LETTERS, POSITION ) ;

                 GO TO START ;
              END EX4_6 ;
```

4.7

```
EX4_7:     PROCEDURE OPTIONS (MAIN) ;

           /* SOLUTION TO EXERCISE 4.7 */

           DECLARE   I FIXED,
                     ( A(10), TEMP ) FLOAT ;

START:     /* READ IN THE NUMBERS TO BE SORTED */
           GET LIST( A ) ;

           /* PRINT THE ORIGINAL LIST */
           PUT LIST( A ) ;

SORT:      /* SORT THE NUMBERS INTO ASCENDING ORDER */
           DO I = 2 BY 1 TO 10 ;
               IF A(I-1)>A(I) THEN
                  DO ;
                      /* TRANSPOSE THE NUMBERS */
                      TEMP = A(I) ;
                      A(I) = A(I-1) ;
                      A(I-1) = TEMP ;
                      GO TO SORT ;
                  END ;
           END ;

           /* PRINT THE SORTED LIST */
           PUT LIST( A ) ;

           /* REVERSE THE ARRAY */
           DO I = 1 BY 1 TO 5 ;
              TEMP= A(I) ;
              A(I) = A(11-I) ;
              A(11-I) = TEMP ;
           END ;

           /* PRINT THE NEW LIST */
           PUT LIST( A ) ;

           GO TO START ;
       END EX4_7 ;
```

4.8

```
EX4_8:    PROCEDURE OPTIONS (MAIN) ;

            /* SOLUTION TO EXERCISE 4.8 */

            DECLARE ( X, TX ) FLOAT ;

            DO X = -3 BY 0.5 TO 3 ;

                /* ESTABLISH DENOMINATOR */
                TX = X**2 - 1 ;

                IF TX=0 THEN /* DO NOT DIVIDE */
                    PUT LIST( 'X = ', X,
                            ' CAUSES DIVISION BY ZERO.' ) ;
                ELSE PUT LIST( X, X/TX ) ;
            END ;
        END EX4_8 ;
```

5. 1

```
EX5_1:    PROCEDURE OPTIONS (MAIN) ;

          /* SOLUTION TO EXERCISE 5.1 */

          DECLARE 1 JOB_ACCOUNT,
                    2 ACCOUNT_NUMBER  FIXED,
                    2 FUNDS           FIXED(8,2),
                    2 TIME,
                     3 COMPILE        FLOAT,
                     3 EXECUTE        FLOAT,
                    2 RATE            FIXED(5,2) ;

START:    GET LIST( JOB_ACCOUNT ) ;
          FUNDS = FUNDS - RATE*(EXECUTE + 0.5*COMPILE) ;

          PUT LIST( JOB_ACCOUNT ) ;

          GO TO START ;
          END EX5_1 ;
```

5. 2 A.S.T will be assigned the value of B. S. T. In order to

modify A.V. W the statement must be A. V = B, BY NAME ;

5. 3

```
EX5_3:    PROCEDURE OPTIONS (MAIN) ;

          /* SOLUTION TO EXERCISE 5.3 */

          DECLARE 1 BOOKS,
                    2 FICTION,
                    (3 NOVELS(275),
                     3 SHORT_STORIES(200)) CHARACTER(10),
                    2 NON_FICTION,
                    (3 BIOGRAPHY(125),
                     3 DOCUMENTARY(70),
                     3 GEN_REFERENCE(100)) CHARACTER(10) ;
```

```
                     DECLARE TITLE CHARACTER(20) ;

START:               GET LIST( TITLE ) ;

                     IF TITLE='FICTION' THEN
                        PUT LIST( FICTION ) ;
                     ELSE
                     IF TITLE='NONFICTION' THEN
                        PUT LIST( NON_FICTION ) ;
                     ELSE
                     IF TITLE='NOVELS' THEN
                        PUT LIST( NOVELS ) ;
                     ELSE
                     IF TITLE='SHORT STORIES' THEN
                        PUT LIST( SHORT_STORIES ) ;
                     ELSE
                     IF TITLE='BIOGRAPHY' THEN
                        PUT LIST( BIOGRAPHY ) ;
                     ELSE
                     IF TITLE='DOCUMENTARY' THEN
                        PUT LIST( DOCUMENTARY ) ;
                     ELSE
                     IF TITLE='REFERENCE' THEN
                        PUT LIST( GEN_REFERENCE ) ;
                     GO TO START ;

                 END EX5_3 ;
```

6.1　The ways in which a value can be assigned to a character

string variable are

    1.　By direct assignment (assignment statement)

    2.　By the INITIAL attribute

    3.　By a GET statement

    4.　By a PUT statement with the STRING option

6.2

```
EX6_2:    PROCEDURE OPTIONS (MAIN) ;

          /* SOLUTION TO EXERCISE 6.2 */

          DECLARE (TYPE, SIDE1, SIDE2, SIDE3) FLOAT ;

START:    GET LIST(SIDE1, SIDE2, SIDE3) ;
          IF SIDE1=0 THEN GO TO DONE ;

          /* ASSUME TRIANGLE IS NEITHER ISOSCELES NOR
             EQUILATERAL. */
          TYPE = 0 ;

          /* SET TYPE TO 1 IF NECESSARY. */
          IF (SIDE1=SIDE2) |
             (SIDE1=SIDE3) |
             (SIDE2=SIDE3)
             THEN TYPE = 1 ;

          /* PRINT DATA AND RESULTS */
          PUT DATA(SIDE1, SIDE2, SIDE3, TYPE) ;
          GO TO START ; /* PROCESS NEXT CASE. */
DONE:     END EX6_2 ;
```

6.3   Data-directed input would be awkward in Example No. 20

because the data item names on the input file must be fully

qualified. This requirement would make the data extremely

difficult to prepare. There would be no particular dis-

advantage to using data-directed output.

6.4   Data-directed output would be particularly useful in

Example No. 13, because the output would be easily

readable, e.g.,

$$NAME(1, 2, 3, 4) = JOHN\ JONES$$

which indicates quite clearly that the name John Jones is

associated with extension 1234. The results might be

further clarified if the array had been named EXTENSION

instead of NAME.

6.5

```
EX6_5:     PROCEDURE OPTIONS (MAIN) ;

           /* SOLUTION TO EXERCISE 6.5 */

           DECLARE  A1(10)    FIXED(10),
                    A2(10)    FLOAT(5),
                    KEY       CHARACTER(1),
                    I         FIXED ;

START:     /* READ THE FIRST CHARACTER */
           GET EDIT( KEY )( A(1) ) COPY ;
```

```
START2:        IF KEY='A' THEN
                  GET EDIT( (A1(I) DO I = 2,4,6,8,10) )
                          ( 5F(10) ) COPY ;
               ELSE IF KEY='B' THEN
                  GET EDIT( A1 ) ( 10F(5) ) COPY ;

               ELSE IF KEY='C' THEN
                  GET EDIT( A2 ) ( 10F(5,2) ) COPY ;

               ELSE IF KEY='D' THEN
                  DO ;
                     GET EDIT( KEY ) ( X(50), A(1) ) COPY ;
                     GO TO START2 ;
                  END ;

               ELSE IF KEY='E' THEN GO TO STOP ;
               GO TO START ;

STOP:     END EX6_5 ;
```

7.1

```
EX7_1:    PROCEDURE OPTIONS (MAIN) ;

              /* SOLUTION TO EXERCISE 7.1 */


MMULT:    PROCEDURE( A, B, C ) ;

              DECLARE   ( A, B, C )(15,15) FLOAT,
                        ( I, J, K ) FIXED BINARY,
                        SUM FLOAT ;

              DO I = 1 TO 15 ;
                 DO J = 1 TO 15 ;

                    SUM = 0 ;

                    DO K = 1 TO 15 ;
                        SUM = SUM + A(I,K)*B(K,J) ;
                    END ;

                    C(I,J) = SUM ;

                 END ;
              END ;

              RETURN ;

          END MMULT ;


              DECLARE   ( X, Y, Z )(15,15) FLOAT ;
START:        GET LIST( X, Y ) ;
              CALL MMULT( X, Y, Z ) ;
              PUT EDIT( ((X(I,J) DO J = 1 TO 15) DO I = 1 TO 15) )
                        (PAGE, 15( 15E(15,6), SKIP) )
                        ( ((Y(I,J) DO J = 1 TO 15) DO I = 1 TO 15) )
                        (PAGE, 15( 15E(15,6), SKIP) )
                        ( ((Z(I,J) DO J = 1 TO 15) DO I = 1 TO 15) )
                        (PAGE, 15( 15E(15,6), SKIP) ) ;

              GO TO START ;

          END EX7_1 ;
```

7.3 The non-recursive function shown below with a driver program is much more efficient than the recursive function shown on page 231, because it will execute much faster: for each multiplication in the following function, the recursive function uses one multiplication and one procedure call

```
EX7_3:    PROCEDURE OPTIONS (MAIN) ;
               /* SOLUTION TO EXERCISE 7.3 */

FACT: PROCEDURE( N ) FIXED ;
          /* SOLUTION TO EXERCISE 7.3 -
             NON-RECURSIVE FACTORIAL */

          DECLARE ( N, I, F ) FIXED ;

          F = 1 ;

          DO I = 2 TO N ;
             F = F*I ;
          END ;

          RETURN( F ) ;
      END FACT ;

          DECLARE FACT ENTRY( FIXED )  RETURNS( FIXED ) ;

          DO I = 1 TO 6 ;
             PUT SKIP LIST( FACT(I) ) ;
          END ;

      END EX7_3 ;
```

```
EX7_4:    PROCEDURE OPTIONS (MAIN) ;

               /* SOLUTION TO EXERCISE 7.4 */


POLY: PROCEDURE( A, N, X ) FLOAT ;

          /* SOLUTION TO EXERCISE 7.4 */

          DECLARE   A(0:20) FLOAT, /* COEFFICIENTS */
                    N FIXED, /* DEGREE OF POLYNOMIAL */
                    X FLOAT,  /* VALUE OF VARIABLE */
                    I FIXED,

                    ( VAL,          /* EVALUATED POLYNOMIAL */
                      TX ) FLOAT ;

          VAL = A(0) ; /* INITIALIZE VALUE */
          TX = 1 ;     /* 'TX' AVOIDS EXPONENTIATION */

          DO I = 1 TO N ;

             TX = TX*X ; /* NEXT POWER OF X  */

             /* ADD NEXT TERM */
             VAL = VAL + A(I)*TX ;

          END ;

          RETURN( VAL ) ;

        END POLY ;

               DECLARE  ( X(0:20), Y ) FLOAT,
                        ( N, I ) FIXED ;

               DECLARE  POLY ENTRY( (*)FLOAT, FIXED, FLOAT )
                             RETURNS( FLOAT ) ;

START:         GET LIST( N, (X(I) DO I = 0 TO N) ) COPY ;

               DO Y = 0 BY .1 TO 1 ;
                  PUT EDIT( POLY( X, N, Y ) )
                             ( SKIP(2), E(16,8) ) ;
               END ;

               GO TO START ;

             END EX7_4 ;
```

```
EX7_5:    PROCEDURE OPTIONS (MAIN) ;

              /* SOLUTION TO EXERCISE 7.5 */


SORT: PROCEDURE( RECORD ) ;

          /* SOLUTION TO EXERCISE 7.5 -
             SORT DATA RECORDS IN AN
             ARRAY OF STRUCTURES. */

          DECLARE 1 RECORD(100),
                    2 NAME,
                    (3 LAST,
                     3 FIRST) CHARACTER(12),
                     3 MIDDLE CHARACTER(2),
                    2 NUMBER   FIXED,
                        /* 'NUMBER' IS THE SORT KEY */
                   (2 OLD_BAL,
                    2 SER_CHG,
                    2 NEW_BAL) FLOAT,

                    1 TEMP, /* TEMP STORAGE FOR SORT */
                    2 T1,
                    (3 T2,
                     3 T3) CHARACTER(12),
                     3 T4   CHARACTER(2),
                    2 T5    FIXED,
                   (2 T6,
                    2 T7,
                    2 T8)  FLOAT,
                   (I, K) FIXED ;

        DO K = 100 BY -1 TO 2 ;
           DO I = 2 BY 1 TO K ;
              IF NUMBER(I)<NUMBER(I-1) THEN
                 DO ;

                     /* TRANSPOSE RECORDS */
                     TEMP = RECORD(I) ;
                     RECORD(I) = RECORD(I-1) ;
                     RECORD(I-1) = TEMP ;

                 END ;
           END ;
        END ;
        RETURN ;

      END SORT ;
```

```
          DECLARE   1 ACCOUNT(100),
                    2 NAME,
                    (3 LAST,
                     3 FIRST) CHARACTER(12),
                     3 MID    CHARACTER(2),
                    2 NO      FIXED,
                    (2 OLD,
                    2 SER,
                    2 NEW)     FLOAT ;

     GET LIST( ACCOUNT ) ;

     CALL SORT( ACCOUNT ) ;

     PUT PAGE ;
     DO I = 1 TO 100 ;
        PUT SKIP LIST( NO(I), LAST(I), OLD(I),
                       SER(I), NEW(I) ) ;
     END ;

 END EX7_5 ;
```

8. 1

```
EX8_1:     PROCEDURE OPTIONS (MAIN) ;
           /* SOLUTION TO EXERCISE 8.1 */


MMULT:     PROCEDURE( A, B, C, N ) ;
           /* SOLUTION TO EXERCISE 8.1 */

           DECLARE   ( A, B, C )(N,N) FLOAT,
                     ( I, J, K, N ) FIXED,
                     SUM FLOAT ;

           DO I = 1 TO N ;
             DO J = 1 TO N ;

               SUM = 0 ;

               DO K = 1 TO N ;
                   SUM = SUM + A(I,K)*B(K,J) ;
               END ;

               C(I,J) = SUM ;

             END ;

           END ;

         END MMULT ;


           DECLARE N FIXED ;

START:     GET LIST (N) ;

B:         BEGIN ;

               DECLARE ( X, Y, Z )(N,N) FLOAT ;

               GET LIST( X, Y ) ;

               CALL MMULT ( X, Y, Z, N ) ;
```

358

```
          PUT EDIT( ((X(I,J) DO J = 1 TO N) DO I = 1 TO N) )
                  (PAGE, (N) ( (N) E(15,6), SKIP) )
                ( ((Y(I,J) DO J = 1 TO N) DO I = 1 TO N) )
                  (PAGE, (N) ( (N) E(15,6), SKIP) )
                ( ((Z(I,J) DO J = 1 TO N) DO I = 1 TO N) )
                  (PAGE, (N) ( (N) E(15,6), SKIP) ) ;

    END ;

    GO TO START ;

END EX8_1 ;
```

9.1   In P1, the effective on-unit for OVERFLOW at the time the statement at X is executed is the standard system action. The first on-unit, GO TO Y, is overridden by the second one, GO TO Z, in the outer block. The on-unit in the BEGIN block is stacked on the latter unit; the first REVERT statement re-establishes GO TO Z. The second REVERT statement has no effect; only those conditions enabled within a block may be REVERTed within that block.

In P2, the effective on-unit for OVERFLOW at the time the statement at X is executed is GO TO Y. The on-unit established in the BEGIN block is active only while execution is in the block.

10.1

```
EX10_1:   PROCEDURE OPTIONS (MAIN) ;

          /* SOLUTION TO EXERCISE 10.1 -
             REVERSE A CHARACTER STRING */

          DECLARE   STRING      CHARACTER(20) VARYING,
                    TEMP        CHARACTER(1),
                    ( I, CHARS ) FIXED ;

START:    /* READ STRING */
          GET LIST( STRING ) ;

          /* PRINT INPUT STRING */
          PUT SKIP(2) LIST( STRING ) ;

          /* REVERSE THE STRING */

          CHARS = LENGTH( STRING ) ;

          DO I = CHARS/2 BY -1 TO 1 ;

             TEMP = SUBSTR( STRING,I,1 ) ;

             SUBSTR( STRING,I,1 ) =
                 SUBSTR( STRING,CHARS+1-I,1 ) ;

             SUBSTR( STRING,CHARS+1-I,1 ) = TEMP ;

          END ;

          /* PRINT RESULTS */
          PUT SKIP LIST( STRING ) ;

          GO TO START ;
       END EX10_1 ;
```

10.2

```
EX10_2:   PROCEDURE OPTIONS (MAIN) ;

          /* SOLUTION TO EXERCISE 10.2 -
             PRINT FIRST NONBLANK CHARACTER */

          DECLARE   STRING   CHARACTER(100) VARYING,
                    I        FIXED ;

START:    /* READ STRING */
          GET LIST( STRING ) ;

          /* FIND FIRST NONBLANK CHARACTER */
          DO I = 1 BY 1
               WHILE( SUBSTR( STRING,I,1 ) = ' ' ) ;
          END ;

          /* PRINT ORIGINAL STRING AND RESULTS */
          PUT SKIP LIST( STRING ) ;
          PUT SKIP LIST( SUBSTR( STRING,I,1 ) ) ;

          GO TO START ;
          END EX10_2 ;
```

10.3

```
EX10_3:   PROCEDURE OPTIONS (MAIN) ;

          /* SOLUTION TO EXERCISE 10.3 -
             DELETE BLANKS FROM A STRING */

          DECLARE   TEXT   CHARACTER(200) VARYING,
                    POS    FIXED ;

          ON ENDFILE GO TO EOJ ;

START:    /* READ STRING */
          GET LIST( TEXT ) COPY ;

          /* DELETE BLANKS */

          POS = INDEX( TEXT,' ' ) ;

          DO WHILE( (POS¬=0) ) ;

              TEXT = SUBSTR( TEXT,1,POS-1 ) ||
                     SUBSTR( TEXT, POS+1 ) ;

              POS = INDEX( TEXT,' ' ) ;
```

```
                  END ;

                  /* PRINT RESULTS */
                  PUT LIST( TEXT ) ;

                  GO TO START ;
        EOJ:      END EX10_3 ;
```

10.4

```
    EX10_4:   PROCEDURE OPTIONS (MAIN) ;

              /* SOLUTION TO EXERCISE 10.4 */

              DECLARE  (TEXT, WORD)   CHARACTER(200) VARYING,
                        P              FIXED ;

              ON ENDFILE GO TO EOJ ;

    START:    /* READ STRING */
              GET LIST( TEXT ) COPY ;

    NEXT:     /* GET THE FIRST (OR NEXT) WORD */
              DO P = 1 TO LENGTH( TEXT )
                    WHILE( INDEX( '.,; ',
                                      SUBSTR(TEXT,P,1) ) =0 ) ;
              END ;
              WORD = SUBSTR( TEXT,1,P ) ;

              /* IS FIRST CHARACTER 'A' -- */
              IF SUBSTR( WORD,1,1 )='A' THEN
                 PUT LIST( WORD ) ;

              /* EXAMINE NEXT WORD */
              TEXT = SUBSTR( TEXT,P+1 ) ;
              IF TEXT = '' THEN  GO TO START ;
              GO TO NEXT ;

    EOJ:    END EX10_4 ;
```

```
EX10_5:   PROCEDURE OPTIONS (MAIN) ;

               /* SOLUTION TO EXERCISE 10.5 */

               DECLARE   TEXT   CHARACTER(200) VARYING,
                         CHAR   CHARACTER(1),
                         (SENT,   /* NO. OF SENTENCES */
                          WORDS,  /* NO. OF WORDS */
                          LETTERS)  FIXED ;

START:         /* INITIALIZE AND READ TEXT */
               SENT, WORDS, LETTERS = 0 ;
               GET LIST( TEXT ) ;

               /* EXAMINE TEXT FOR WORDS AND SENTENCES, AND
                  COUNT LETTERS IN THE PROCESS */

               DO I = 1 BY 1 TO LENGTH( TEXT ) ;
                  CHAR = SUBSTR( TEXT, I, 1 ) ;
                  IF CHAR='.' THEN
                     DO ;
                         /* A PERIOD ENDS A WORD AND A SENT. */
                         WORDS = WORDS + 1 ;
                         SENT = SENT + 1 ;
                     END ;
                  ELSE IF CHAR=' ' THEN WORDS = WORDS + 1 ;
                  ELSE   LETTERS = LETTERS + 1 ;

                  /* NOTE THE ASSUMPTION THAT A CHARACTER IS
                     CONSIDERED TO BE A LETTER IF IT IS NOT
                     A PERIOD OR A BLANK. */

               END ;

               /* PRINT RESULTS */
               PUT SKIP EDIT( 'SENTENCES =', SENT,
                              'WORDS/SENTENCE =', WORDS/SENT,
                              'LETTERS/WORD =', LETTERS/WORDS )
                            ( X(10), A, F(4) ) ;
               GO TO START ;
            END EX10_5 ;
```

```
EX10_6:   PROCEDURE OPTIONS (MAIN) ;

          /* SOLUTION TO EXERCISE 10.6 */

          DECLARE  ( ENG, WORD ) CHARACTER (200) VARYING,
                   PIG            CHARACTER (400) VARYING,
                   (FIRST,    /* FIRST CHARACTER IN WORD */
                    LAST,     /* LAST CHARACTER IN WORD */
                    VOL,      /* POSITION IN WORD OF VOWEL */
                    FLAG,     /* '.,;' IN WORD */
                    LW,       /* LENGTH OF A WORD */
                    I ) FIXED ;

          ON ENDFILE  GO TO FIN ;

START:    GET LIST( ENG ) COPY ;

          PIG = '' ;
          I = 1 ;

          /* SCAN FOR FIRST NON BLANK CHARACTER */
TOP:      DO FIRST = I TO LENGTH( ENG )
                    WHILE( SUBSTR(ENG, FIRST, 1) = ' ' ) ;
          END ;

          IF FIRST >= LENGTH( ENG )  THEN GO TO PRINT ;

          FLAG = 0 ;
          /* SCAN FOR A BLANK */
          DO LAST = FIRST + 1 TO LENGTH( ENG )
                    WHILE( SUBSTR( ENG, LAST, 1 )¬=' ' ) ;
          END ;

          /* CHARACTERS TO BE CONVERTED ARE PUT INTO WORD */
          WORD = SUBSTR(ENG, FIRST, LAST-FIRST) ;

          LW = LENGTH( WORD ) ;
          IF INDEX( '.,;', SUBSTR( WORD, LW, 1 ) ) ¬= 0
             THEN  DO ;
                      FLAG = 1 ;
                      LW = LW - 1 ;
                   END ;

          /* SCAN FOR VOWEL */
          DO VOL = 1 TO LW
                    WHILE( INDEX( 'AEIOU',
                                  SUBSTR( WORD, VOL, 1) )
                          =0 ) ;
          END ;

          PIG = PIG || SUBSTR( WORD, VOL, LW-VOL+1 ) ||
                SUBSTR( WORD, 1, VOL-1) || 'AY' ;

          IF FLAG   THEN
             PIG = PIG || SUBSTR( WORD, LW+1) ;
```

```
           PIG = PIG || ' ' ;
           I = LAST + 1 ;
           GO TO TOP ;

PRINT:     PUT SKIP LIST( PIG ) ;
           GO TO START ;

FIN:    END EX10_6 ;
```

INDEX

370

Logical
>construction, 42, 56
>errors, 56, 245, 256
>expressions, 39, 57
>operators, 38-39
>>strength of, 40
>record, 300-301
>sequence, 25
>statement, 25

Loop, 113-124
>characteristics of, 119
>nested, 120

MAIN option, 203, 227
Main procedure, 202

Null
>on-unit, 251
>statement, 50-51
>string, 77

Object program, 24
On-unit, 247, 251
>null, 251
>redefinition of, 251
ON statement, 246-247, 260
>canceling of, 251
>overriding of, 249
>stacking of, 251
OPEN statement, 282-283, 302
>with IDENT option, 285
Operands, 13
Operating system, 246, 252
Operators, 316
>arithmetic, 11
>>strength of, 12
>assignment, 18
>comparison, 37-38
>logical, 38-39
>>strength of, 40
>relational, 37-38
>string, 271

Output,
>see "I/O"
OUTPUT attribute, 281
OVERFLOW condition, 245, 327

Padding, 265
PAGE,
>format phrase, 187
>option, 185
Parameters, 205
>actual, 208-209
>arrays as, 215
>formal, 208
>name, 210
>structures as, 216
>value, 210
Physical record, 291, 295
PICTURE
>attribute, 73-76
>>for arithmetic
>>data, 74
>>for character
>>data, 82-83
>specification characters,
>>172, 329-332
>>drifting, 175
Pointer variables, 304-305
Precision,
>attribute, 66, 68
>of data, 15
Prefixes, 253-254, 255
PRINT attribute, 280, 281
PROCEDURE statement, 4
>with MAIN option, 203,
>>227
Procedures, 202
>arguments to, 208
>declaration of, 205, 207
>>220
>external, 227
>function, 210, 213
>internal, 227, 234

Procedures (cont.)
main, 202
nesting of, 226
parameters to, 205-206
recursive, 231
subroutine, 210-213
Process block, 33
Program, 1
main, 202
object, 24
phases of, 25, 156
source, 25
structure of, 25, 227
sub-, see "Procedures"
Program library, 230
Programmer-defined
conditions, 259-260
Pseudo-variable, 270
PUT statement, 7, 157
with options,
FILE, 280
LINE, 185
PAGE, 185
SKIP, 185
STRING, 195, 196

Qualification operator, 142,
316
Qualified names, 142, 143
expressions with, 144
in I/O, 166

READ statement, 296
with KEY, 309
with SET, 305
REAL attribute, 92
Recommended practices
buffering, 301
indentation
DO, 55-56
structures, 138

Recommended practices (cont.)
labeling DO loops, 115
loops, construction of, 121
minimizing round off
error, 129-130
PICTURE effect on
execution, 76
use of Entry and
RETURNS, 221-222,
230-231
use of CHECK, 257
Record
physical, 291
logical, 300-301
keys, 307
RECORD attribute, 295
RECURSIVE attribute, 231
Relational operators, 37, 38,
316
Remote format specifica-
tions, 197
Repetitive specifications,
188-191
Replication factor
in constants, 75, 78, 84
in formats, 176, 178
RETURN statement, 206, 213
RETURNS attribute, 221
REVERT statement, 251-252
Roundoff error, 129-130
Row major order, 109-111

Scale attribute, 69
Scientific notation, 14
Scope
of group, 56
of identifiers, 222-226,
235, 241
of loop, 123
of prefixes, 254
Search argument, 273

373